THE
BIBLE
HEALING SCRIPTURES

OLD AND NEW TESTAMENT EXTRACTS

Authorised King James Version

Healing Stories and Sections Compiled from the King James Bible in the order of the Books. Suggested Prayers added for each Section.

Grosvenor House
Publishing Limited

THIS

BIBLE

HEALING SCRIPTURES

IS PRESENTED TO

_____

BY

_____

_____

ON

_____

_____

Who his own self bare our sins in his own body on the tree, that we, being dead to sins, should live unto righteousness: by whose stripes ye were healed.
1 Peter 2:24

All rights reserved
Copyright © Dr Timothy O., 2025

The right of Dr Timothy O. to be identified as the author of this
work has been asserted in accordance with Section 78
of the Copyright, Designs and Patents Act 1988

The book cover is copyright to Dr Timothy O.

This book is published by Grosvenor House
Publishing Ltd Link House,
140 The Broadway, Tolworth, Surrey, KT6 7HT.
www.grosvenorhousepublishing.co.uk

This book is sold subject to the conditions that it shall not, by way of trade
or otherwise, be lent, resold, hired out or otherwise circulated without the
author's or publisher's prior consent in any form of binding or cover other
than that in which it is published and without a similar condition including
this condition being imposed on the subsequent purchaser.

This book is protected under copyright law. Copyright belongs to
Dr Timothy O. with license from Cambridge University Press to
produce the Authorised (Kings James) Bible extracts.

Rights in the Authorized (King James) Version in the United Kingdom are
vested in the Crown. Reproduced by permission of the Crown's patentee,
Cambridge University Press.

A CIP record for this book
is available from the British Library

Paperback ISBN 978-1-83615-328-3
Hardback ISBN 978-1-83615-329-0
eBook ISBN 978-1-83615-330-6

PREFACE

The selection of healing verses was assembled and chronologically ordered in line with the Authorised King James version of the Bible.

This book contains a collection of exact Bible verses relating directly or indirectly to the subject of healing that have been documented as healing events, information or doctrine in the Authorised King James version of the Bible. Each group of verses are referred to as sections.

The prayers at the end of each section are simply prayer suggestions which you can speak, recite or repeat. These prayers are constructed based on the author's understanding of the Bible healing section in question.

Majority of the prayer suggestion are written from a first person position personalised to the readers; however, it can be used in plurality for both readers and others or just for others.

According to the content of the Bible, all prayer must be said in the name of Jesus. Remember to give thanks after each prayer especially if thanks are not included in prayer suggestion.

Every reader who decides to use the prayer suggestions will be fully responsible for such decision.

CONTENTS

HEALINGS FROM THE OLD TESTAMENT

Confessions Of Healing Bible Verses	i
Genesis	1
Exodus	9
Leviticus	15
Numbers	21
Deuteronomy	27
Joshua	33
Judges	37
Ruth	43
1 Samuel	47
2 Samuel	53
1 Kings	59
2 Kings	65
1 Chronicles	77
2 Chronicles	81
Ezra	85
Nehemiah	89
Esther	93
Job	97
Psalms	103
Proverbs	113
Ecclesiastes	123
Song of Solomon	127

Isaiah	131
Jeremiah	141
Lamentations	149
Ezekiel	155
Daniel	161
Hosea	165
Joel	171
Amos	177
Obadiah	181
Jonah	185
Micah	191
Nahum	195
Habakkuk	199
Zephaniah	203
Haggai	207
Zechariah	211
Malachi	217

HEALINGS FROM THE NEW TESTAMENT

Matthew	223
Mark	251
Luke	277
John	311
Acts	319
Romans	337
1 Corinthians	341
2 Corinthians	347

Galatians	351
Ephesians	357
Philippians	367
Colossians	373
1 Thessalonians	377
2 Thessalonians	381
1 Timothy	385
2 Timothy	389
Titus	393
Philemon	397
Hebrews	401
James	413
1 Peter	421
2 Peter	427
1 John	431
2 John	437
3 John	441
Jude	445
Revelation	449

VERSES ON PRAYER, CONFESSIONS & AUTHORITY

Short verses on healing	455
Short verses on faith	458
Short verses on rebuking the devil	464
Short verses on patience	469

Confessions Of Healing Bible Verses

Exodus 15:26b

I will put none of these diseases upon thee, which I have brought upon the Egyptians: for I am the Lord that healeth thee.

Exodus 23:25

And ye shall serve the Lord your God, and he shall bless thy bread, and thy water; and I will take sickness away from the midst of thee.

Exodus 23:26

There shall nothing cast their young, nor be barren, in thy land: the number of thy days I will fulfil.

Deuteronomy 7:15

And the Lord will take away from thee all sickness, and will put none of the evil diseases of Egypt, which thou knowest, upon thee; but will lay them upon all them that hate thee.

2 Kings 20:5b KJV

I have heard thy prayer, I have seen thy tears: behold, I will heal thee: on the third day thou shalt go up unto the house of the LORD.

Isaiah 38:16

O Lord, by these things men live, and in all these things is the life of my spirit: so wilt thou recover me, and make me to live.

Isaiah 53:4-5

Surely he hath borne our griefs, and carried our sorrows: yet we did esteem him stricken, smitten of God, and afflicted. [5] But he was wounded for our transgressions, he was bruised for our iniquities: the chastisement of our peace was upon him; and with his stripes we are healed.

Isaiah 54:17

No weapon that is formed against thee shall prosper; and every tongue that shall rise against thee in judgment thou shalt condemn. This is the heritage of the servants of the Lord, and their righteousness is of me, saith the Lord.

Isaiah 57:18

I have seen his ways, and will heal him: I will lead him also, and restore comforts unto him and to his mourners.

Isaiah 58:8

Then shall thy light break forth as the morning, and thine health shall spring forth speedily: and thy righteousness shall go before thee; the glory of the Lord shall be thy rereward.

Matthew 8:17

That it might be fulfilled which was spoken by Esaias the prophet, saying, Himself took our infirmities, and bare our sicknesses.

Matthew 17:20b

If ye have faith as a grain of mustard seed, ye shall say unto this mountain, Remove hence to yonder place; and it shall remove; and nothing shall be impossible unto you.

Mark 9:23

Jesus said unto him, If thou canst believe, all things are possible to him that believeth.

Mark 10:27

And Jesus looking upon them saith, With men it is impossible, but not with God: for with God all things are possible.

Mark 11:23

For verily I say unto you, That whosoever shall say unto this mountain, Be thou removed, and be thou cast into the sea; and shall not doubt in his heart, but shall believe that those things which he saith shall come to pass; he shall have whatsoever he saith.

1 Peter 2:24

Who his own self bare our sins in his own body on the tree, that we, being dead to sins, should live unto righteousness: by whose stripes ye were healed.

1 Peter 5:9

Whom resist stedfast in the faith, knowing that the same afflictions are accomplished in your brethren that are in the world.

1 John 4:4

Ye are of God, little children, and have overcome them: because greater is he that is in you, than he that is in the world.

1 John 5:4

For whatsoever is born of God overcometh the world: and this is the victory that overcometh the world, even our faith.

3 John 1:2

Beloved, I wish above all things that thou mayest prosper and be in health, even as thy soul prospereth.

Revelation 12:11

And they overcame him by the blood of the Lamb, and by the word of their testimony; and they loved not their lives unto the death.

THE OLD TESTAMENT

HEALINGS FROM THE BOOK OF
GENESIS

Abimelech's Wife

Genesis 20:1-8

1 And Abraham journeyed from thence toward the south country, and dwelled between Kadesh and Shur, and sojourned in Gerar.

2 And Abraham said of Sarah his wife, She is my sister: and Abimelech king of Gerar sent, and took Sarah.

3 But God came to Abimelech in a dream by night, and said to him, Behold, thou art but a dead man, for the woman which thou hast taken; for she is a man's wife.

4 But Abimelech had not come near her: and he said, Lord, wilt thou slay also a righteous nation?

5 Said he not unto me, She is my sister? and she, even she herself said, He is my brother: in the integrity of my heart and innocency of my hands have I done this.

6 And God said unto him in a dream, Yea, I know that thou didst this in the integrity of thy heart; for I also withheld thee from sinning against me: therefore suffered I thee not to touch her.

7 Now therefore restore the man his wife; for he is a prophet, and he shall pray for thee, and thou shalt live: and if thou restore her not, know thou that thou shalt surely die, thou, and all that are thine.

8 Therefore Abimelech rose early in the morning, and called all

contd.

Genesis 20:9-14 — *Abimelech's Wife*

his servants, and told all these things in their ears: and the men were sore afraid.

9 Then Abimelech called Abraham, and said unto him, What hast thou done unto us? and what have I offended thee, that thou hast brought on me and on my kingdom a great sin? thou hast done deeds unto me that ought not to be done.

10 And Abimelech said unto Abraham, What sawest thou, that thou hast done this thing?

11 And Abraham said, Because I thought, Surely the fear of God is not in this place; and they will slay me for my wife's sake.

12 And yet indeed she is my sister; she is the daughter of my father, but not the daughter of my mother; and she became my wife.

13 And it came to pass, when God caused me to wander from my father's house, that I said unto her, This is thy kindness which thou shalt shew unto me; at every place whither we shall come, say of me, He is my brother.

14 And Abimelech took sheep, and oxen, and menservants, and women servants, and gave them unto Abraham, and restored him Sarah his wife.

contd.

Abimelech's Wife — **Genesis 20:15-17**

15 And Abimelech said, Behold, my land is before thee: dwell where it pleaseth thee.

16 And unto Sarah he said, Behold, I have given thy brother a thousand pieces of silver: behold, he is to thee a covering of the eyes, unto all that are with thee, and with all other: thus she was reproved.

17 So Abraham prayed unto God: and God healed Abimelech, and his wife, and his maidservants; and they bare children.

Prayer:

Dear Lord reveal to me and help me straighten areas in my life where I need to make amends, and heal me

Genesis 21:14-19 *Hagar And Her Son*

14 And Abraham rose up early in the morning, and took bread, and a bottle of water, and gave it unto Hagar, putting it on her shoulder, and the child, and sent her away: and she departed, and wandered in the wilderness of Beersheba.

15 And the water was spent in the bottle, and she cast the child under one of the shrubs.

16 And she went, and sat her down over against him a good way off, as it were a bow shot: for she said, Let me not see the death of the child. And she sat over against him, and lift up her voice, and wept.

17 And God heard the voice of the lad; and the angel of God called to Hagar out of heaven, and said unto her, What aileth thee, Hagar? fear not; for God hath heard the voice of the lad where he is.

18 Arise, lift up the lad, and hold him in thine hand; for I will make him a great nation.

19 And God opened her eyes, and she saw a well of water; and she went, and filled the bottle with water, and gave the lad drink.

Prayer:

Merciful Father in this pain, reveal to me the well of your healing power in your word that I may drink

Jacob And His Sons

Genesis 43:23-28

23 And he said, Peace be to you, fear not: your God, and the God of your father, hath given you treasure in your sacks: I had your money. And he brought Simeon out unto them.

24 And the man brought the men into Joseph's house, and gave them water, and they washed their feet; and he gave their asses provender.

25 And they made ready the present against Joseph came at noon: for they heard that they should eat bread there.

26 And when Joseph came home, they brought him the present which was in their hand into the house, and bowed themselves to him to the earth.

27 And he asked them of their welfare, and said, Is your father well, the old man of whom ye spake? Is he yet alive?

28 And they answered, Thy servant our father is in good health, he is yet alive. And they bowed down their heads, and made obeisance.

Prayer:

O God of heaven and earth, I receive and thank you for good health and long life in Christ Jesus

> # HEALINGS FROM THE BOOK OF
EXODUS

The Children Of Israel Exodus 15:22-26

22 So Moses brought Israel from the Red sea, and they went out into the wilderness of Shur; and they went three days in the wilderness, and found no water.

23 And when they came to Marah, they could not drink of the waters of Marah, for they were bitter: therefore the name of it was called Marah.

24 And the people murmured against Moses, saying, What shall we drink?

25 And he cried unto the Lord; and the Lord shewed him a tree, which when he had cast into the waters, the waters were made sweet: there he made for them a statute and an ordinance, and there he proved them,

26 And said, If thou wilt diligently hearken to the voice of the Lord thy God, and wilt do that which is right in his sight, and wilt give ear to his commandments, and keep all his statutes, I will put none of these diseases upon thee, which I have brought upon the Egyptians: for I am the Lord that healeth thee.

Prayer:

Father, help me to diligently hearken to your voice and do what is right in your sight O God who heals me

Exodus 21:18-19 — *The Children Of Israel*

18 And if men strive together, and one smite another with a stone, or with his fist, and he die not, but keepeth his bed:

19 If he rise again, and walk abroad upon his staff, then shall he that smote him be quit: only he shall pay for the loss of his time, and shall cause him to be thoroughly healed.

Prayer:

Our God and King, where I have sustained injuries in my body, I receive healing from your word

The Children Of Israel — Exodus 23:20-25

20 Behold, I send an Angel before thee, to keep thee in the way, and to bring thee into the place which I have prepared.

21 Beware of him, and obey his voice, provoke him not; for he will not pardon your transgressions: for my name is in him.

22 But if thou shalt indeed obey his voice, and do all that I speak; then I will be an enemy unto thine enemies, and an adversary unto thine adversaries.

23 For mine Angel shall go before thee, and bring thee in unto the Amorites, and the Hittites, and the Perizzites, and the Canaanites, the Hivites, and the Jebusites: and I will cut them off.

24 Thou shalt not bow down to their gods, nor serve them, nor do after their works: but thou shalt utterly overthrow them, and quite break down their images.

25 And ye shall serve the Lord your God, and he shall bless thy bread, and thy water; and I will take sickness away from the midst of thee.

Prayer:

O Lord my God I will serve you, and you shall bless my bread and my water, and take sickness away from me

HEALINGS FROM THE BOOK OF LEVITICUS

The Children Of Israel — Leviticus 13:12-18

12 And if a leprosy break out abroad in the skin, and the leprosy cover all the skin of him that hath the plague from his head even to his foot, wheresoever the priest looketh;

13 Then the priest shall consider: and, behold, if the leprosy have covered all his flesh, he shall pronounce him clean that hath the plague: it is all turned white: he is clean.

14 But when raw flesh appeareth in him, he shall be unclean.

15 And the priest shall see the raw flesh, and pronounce him to be unclean: for the raw flesh is unclean: it is a leprosy.

16 Or if the raw flesh turn again, and be changed unto white, he shall come unto the priest;

17 And the priest shall see him: and, behold, if the plague be turned into white; then the priest shall pronounce him clean that hath the plague: he is clean.

18 The flesh also, in which, even in the skin thereof, was a boil, and is healed,

Prayer:

Father I call upon you to heal the boil, disease and growth in my flesh; I believe I receive my healing

Leviticus 13:32-37 — *The Children Of Israel*

32 And in the seventh day the priest shall look on the plague: and, behold, if the scall spread not, and there be in it no yellow hair, and the scall be not in sight deeper than the skin;

33 He shall be shaven, but the scall shall he not shave; and the priest shall shut up him that hath the scall seven days more:

34 And in the seventh day the priest shall look on the scall: and, behold, if the scall be not spread in the skin, nor be in sight deeper than the skin; then the priest shall pronounce him clean: and he shall wash his clothes, and be clean.

35 But if the scall spread much in the skin after his cleansing;

36 Then the priest shall look on him: and, behold, if the scall be spread in the skin, the priest shall not seek for yellow hair; he is unclean.

37 But if the scall be in his sight at a stay, and that there is black hair grown up therein; the scall is healed, he is clean: and the priest shall pronounce him clean.

Prayer:

I thank you Lord for the natural healing process which you have created; I pray you grant me a speedy recovery

The Children Of Israel — Leviticus 14:1-4

1 And the Lord spake unto Moses, saying,

2 This shall be the law of the leper in the day of his cleansing: He shall be brought unto the priest:

3 And the priest shall go forth out of the camp; and the priest shall look, and, behold, if the plague of leprosy be healed in the leper;

4 Then shall the priest command to take for him that is to be cleansed two birds alive and clean, and cedar wood, and scarlet, and hyssop:

Prayer:

Thank you Father, for by the stripes of our Lord Jesus I am healed as the church elders pray over me

Leviticus 14:43-48 — The Children Of Israel

43 And if the plague come again, and break out in the house, after that he hath taken away the stones, and after he hath scraped the house, and after it is plaistered;

44 Then the priest shall come and look, and, behold, if the plague be spread in the house, it is a fretting leprosy in the house; it is unclean.

45 And he shall break down the house, the stones of it, and the timber thereof, and all the morter of the house; and he shall carry them forth out of the city into an unclean place.

46 Moreover he that goeth into the house all the while that it is shut up shall be unclean until the even.

47 And he that lieth in the house shall wash his clothes; and he that eateth in the house shall wash his clothes.

48 And if the priest shall come in, and look upon it, and, behold, the plague hath not spread in the house, after the house was plaistered: then the priest shall pronounce the house clean, because the plague is healed.

Prayer:

Lord I pray that you heal me from the plague that breaks out around me and keep me from it in future

HEALINGS FROM THE BOOK OF
NUMBERS

Moses And Miriam
Numbers 12:10-15

10 And the cloud departed from off the tabernacle; and, behold, Miriam became leprous, white as snow: and Aaron looked upon Miriam, and, behold, she was leprous.

11 And Aaron said unto Moses, Alas, my lord, I beseech thee, lay not the sin upon us, wherein we have done foolishly, and wherein we have sinned.

12 Let her not be as one dead, of whom the flesh is half consumed when he cometh out of his mother's womb.

13 And Moses cried unto the Lord, saying, Heal her now, O God, I beseech thee.

14 And the Lord said unto Moses, If her father had but spit in her face, should she not be ashamed seven days? let her be shut out from the camp seven days, and after that let her be received in again.

15 And Miriam was shut out from the camp seven days: and the people journeyed not till Miriam was brought in again.

Prayer:

Dear Lord I ask for forgiveness where I have given place to the devil and ask that you heal my body

Numbers 16:44-48 — *The Children Of Israel*

44 And the Lord spake unto Moses, saying,

45 Get you up from among this congregation, that I may consume them as in a moment. And they fell upon their faces.

46 And Moses said unto Aaron, Take a censer, and put fire therein from off the altar, and put on incense, and go quickly unto the congregation, and make an atonement for them: for there is wrath gone out from the Lord; the plague is begun.

47 And Aaron took as Moses commanded, and ran into the midst of the congregation; and, behold, the plague was begun among the people: and he put on incense, and made an atonement for the people.

48 And he stood between the dead and the living; and the plague was stayed.

Prayer:

Almighty God, I acknowledge any consequence of my disobedience and ask for forgiveness and healing

The Serpent Of Brass — Numbers 21:5-9

5 And the people spake against God, and against Moses, Wherefore have ye brought us up out of Egypt to die in the wilderness? for there is no bread, neither is there any water; and our soul loatheth this light bread.

6 And the Lord sent fiery serpents among the people, and they bit the people; and much people of Israel died.

7 Therefore the people came to Moses, and said, We have sinned, for we have spoken against the Lord, and against thee; pray unto the Lord, that he take away the serpents from us. And Moses prayed for the people.

8 And the Lord said unto Moses, Make thee a fiery serpent, and set it upon a pole: and it shall come to pass, that every one that is bitten, when he looketh upon it, shall live.

9 And Moses made a serpent of brass, and put it upon a pole, and it came to pass, that if a serpent had bitten any man, when he beheld the serpent of brass, he lived.

Prayer:

O God almighty I look to Jesus as the Israelites looked to the brass serpent and I receive my healing

HEALINGS FROM THE BOOK OF
DEUTERONOMY

God's Promise
Deuteronomy 7:12-15

12 Wherefore it shall come to pass, if ye hearken to these judgments, and keep, and do them, that the Lord thy God shall keep unto thee the covenant and the mercy which he sware unto thy fathers:

13 And he will love thee, and bless thee, and multiply thee: he will also bless the fruit of thy womb, and the fruit of thy land, thy corn, and thy wine, and thine oil, the increase of thy kine, and the flocks of thy sheep, in the land which he sware unto thy fathers to give thee.

14 Thou shalt be blessed above all people: there shall not be male or female barren among you, or among your cattle.

15 And the Lord will take away from thee all sickness, and will put none of the evil diseases of Egypt, which thou knowest, upon thee; but will lay them upon all them that hate thee.

Prayer:

Lord I receive your promise to take away from me all sickness and diseases of the Egyptians

Deuteronomy 28:1-4 — *God's Promise*

1 And it shall come to pass, if thou shalt hearken diligently unto the voice of the Lord thy God, to observe and to do all his commandments which I command thee this day, that the Lord thy God will set thee on high above all nations of the earth:

2 And all these blessings shall come on thee, and overtake thee, if thou shalt hearken unto the voice of the Lord thy God.

3 Blessed shalt thou be in the city, and blessed shalt thou be in the field.

4 Blessed shall be the fruit of thy body, and the fruit of thy ground, and the fruit of thy cattle, the increase of thy kine, and the flocks of thy sheep.

Prayer:

Father, I receive the strength to obey your word and the rewards of health and provision that it bestows

The Children Of Israel — **Deuteronomy 30:17-20**

17 But if thine heart turn away, so that thou wilt not hear, but shalt be drawn away, and worship other gods, and serve them;

18 I denounce unto you this day, that ye shall surely perish, and that ye shall not prolong your days upon the land, whither thou passest over Jordan to go to possess it.

19 I call heaven and earth to record this day against you, that I have set before you life and death, blessing and cursing: therefore choose life, that both thou and thy seed may live:

20 That thou mayest love the Lord thy God, and that thou mayest obey his voice, and that thou mayest cleave unto him: for he is thy life, and the length of thy days: that thou mayest dwell in the land which the Lord sware unto thy fathers, to Abraham, to Isaac, and to Jacob, to give them.

Prayer:

Dear Father I choose life, that both I and my children may live, for you are our lives, and length of our days

Deuteronomy 32:36-39   *The Children Of Israel*

36 For the Lord shall judge his people, and repent himself for his servants, when he seeth that their power is gone, and there is none shut up, or left.

37 And he shall say, Where are their gods, their rock in whom they trusted,

38 Which did eat the fat of their sacrifices, and drank the wine of their drink offerings? let them rise up and help you, and be your protection.

39 See now that I, even I, am he, and there is no god with me: I kill, and I make alive; I wound, and I heal: neither is there any that can deliver out of my hand.

Prayer:

O merciful Lord, I repent of the idolatry in my life and receive Your healing touch and the promise of long life

HEALINGS FROM THE BOOK OF JOSHUA

Book Of The Law   **Joshua 1:6-9**

6 Be strong and of a good courage: for unto this people shalt thou divide for an inheritance the land, which I sware unto their fathers to give them.

7 Only be thou strong and very courageous, that thou mayest observe to do according to all the law, which Moses my servant commanded thee: turn not from it to the right hand or to the left, that thou mayest prosper withersoever thou goest.

8 This book of the law shall not depart out of thy mouth; but thou shalt meditate therein day and night, that thou mayest observe to do according to all that is written therein: for then thou shalt make thy way prosperous, and then thou shalt have good success.

9 Have not I commanded thee? Be strong and of a good courage; be not afraid, neither be thou dismayed: for the Lord thy God is with thee whithersoever thou goest.

Prayer:

Lord help me to read and meditate on your word so that I will make my way prosperous in health and wealth

Joshua 5:6-8 — *The Children Of Israel*

6 For the children of Israel walked forty years in the wilderness, till all the people that were men of war, which came out of Egypt, were consumed, because they obeyed not the voice of the Lord: unto whom the Lord sware that he would not shew them the land, which the Lord sware unto their fathers that he would give us, a land that floweth with milk and honey.

7 And their children, whom he raised up in their stead, them Joshua circumcised: for they were uncircumcised, because they had not circumcised them by the way.

8 And it came to pass, when they had done circumcising all the people, that they abode in their places in the camp, till they were whole.

Prayer:

Almighty Father, may my heart be circumcised through obedience of your word, and my body made whole

HEALINGS FROM THE BOOK OF
JUDGES

9 And when the children of Israel cried unto the Lord, the Lord raised up a deliverer to the children of Israel, who delivered them, even Othniel the son of Kenaz, Caleb's younger brother.

10 And the Spirit of the Lord came upon him, and he judged Israel, and went out to war: and the Lord delivered Chushanrishathaim king of Mesopotamia into his hand; and his hand prevailed against Chushanrishathaim.

11 And the land had rest forty years. And Othniel the son of Kenaz died.

Prayer:

Lord God Almighty, I receive deliverance in my body from the afflictions of the devil

Judges 6:6-9   *The Children Of Israel*

6 And Israel was greatly impoverished because of the Midianites; and the children of Israel cried unto the Lord.

7 And it came to pass, when the children of Israel cried unto the Lord because of the Midianites,

8 That the Lord sent a prophet unto the children of Israel, which said unto them, Thus saith the Lord God of Israel, I brought you up from Egypt, and brought you forth out of the house of bondage;

9 And I delivered you out of the hand of the Egyptians, and out of the hand of all that oppressed you, and drave them out from before you, and gave you their land;

Prayer:

O merciful Lord, I cry out to you for deliverance from sickness and diseases; I claim my deliverance

The Children Of Israel — Judges 11:19-21

19 And Israel sent messengers unto Sihon king of the Amorites, the king of Heshbon; and Israel said unto him, Let us pass, we pray thee, through thy land into my place.

20 But Sihon trusted not Israel to pass through his coast: but Sihon gathered all his people together, and pitched in Jahaz, and fought against Israel.

21 And the Lord God of Israel delivered Sihon and all his people into the hand of Israel, and they smote them: so Israel possessed all the land of the Amorites, the inhabitants of that country.

Prayer:

*O Lord God of Israel, by your might
I receive healing, deliverance and prosperity
as I possess my possession*

HEALINGS FROM THE BOOK OF
RUTH

The Restorer Of Life   **Ruth 4:14-15**

14 And the women said unto Naomi, Blessed be the Lord, which hath not left thee this day without a kinsman, that his name may be famous in Israel.

15 And he shall be unto thee a restorer of thy life, and a nourisher of thine old age: for thy daughter in law, which loveth thee, which is better to thee than seven sons, hath born him.

Prayer:

Like Boaz to Ruth, Jesus is my Kinsman redeemer therefore I am redeemed from all sickness and diseases

HEALINGS FROM THE BOOK OF
1 SAMUEL

The Barren Woman — 1 Samuel 1:10-11; 19-20

10 And she was in bitterness of soul, and prayed unto the Lord, and wept sore.

11 And she vowed a vow, and said, O Lord of hosts, if thou wilt indeed look on the affliction of thine handmaid, and remember me, and not forget thine handmaid, but wilt give unto thine handmaid a man child, then I will give him unto the Lord all the days of his life, and there shall no razor come upon his head.

19 And they rose up in the morning early, and worshipped before the Lord, and returned, and came to their house to Ramah: and Elkanah knew Hannah his wife; and the Lord remembered her.

20 Wherefore it came to pass, when the time was come about after Hannah had conceived, that she bare a son, and called his name Samuel, saying, Because I have asked him of the Lord.

Prayer:

O Lord, just as you remembered Hannah in her affliction, remember me in my affliction

1 Samuel 6:1-3   *The Ark Of The Lord*

1 And the ark of the Lord was in the country of the Philistines seven months.

2 And the Philistines called for the priests and the diviners, saying, What shall we do to the ark of the Lord? tell us wherewith we shall send it to his place.

3 And they said, If ye send away the ark of the God of Israel, send it not empty; but in any wise return him a trespass offering: then ye shall be healed, and it shall be known to you why his hand is not removed from you.

Prayer:

King of Kings and God of heaven and earth, as I offer my praise to you, I receive from you healing in my body

The Restorer Of Life — 1 Samuel 10:17-18

17 And Samuel called the people together unto the Lord to Mizpeh;

18 And said unto the children of Israel, Thus saith the Lord God of Israel, I brought up Israel out of Egypt, and delivered you out of the hand of the Egyptians, and out of the hand of all kingdoms, and of them that oppressed you:

Prayer:

Father, deliver me I pray from the devil's oppression; I claim deliverance from the enemy in my health

HEALINGS FROM THE BOOK OF
2 SAMUEL

The Children Of Israel — 2 Samuel 22:14-18

14 The Lord thundered from heaven, and the most High uttered his voice.

15 And he sent out arrows, and scattered them; lightning, and discomfited them.

16 And the channels of the sea appeared, the foundations of the world were discovered, at the rebuking of the Lord, at the blast of the breath of his nostrils.

17 He sent from above, he took me; he drew me out of many waters;

18 He delivered me from my strong enemy, and from them that hated me: for they were too strong for me.

Prayer:

Father, I claim deliverance from my strong enemy because of the price Jesus has paid for my health

2 Samuel 22:25-28 — The Children Of Israel

25 Therefore the Lord hath recompensed me according to my righteousness; according to my cleanness in his eye sight.

26 With the merciful thou wilt shew thyself merciful, and with the upright man thou wilt shew thyself upright.

27 With the pure thou wilt shew thyself pure; and with the froward thou wilt shew thyself unsavoury.

28 And the afflicted people thou wilt save: but thine eyes are upon the haughty, that thou mayest bring them down.

Prayer:

O most high God, thank you for you are merciful; deliver me from my affliction according to your word

King David And Israel 2 Samuel 24:13-16

13 So Gad came to David, and told him, and said unto him, Shall seven years of famine come unto thee in thy land? or wilt thou flee three months before thine enemies, while they pursue thee? or that there be three days' pestilence in thy land? now advise, and see

14 And David said unto Gad, I am in a great strait: let us fall now into the hand of the Lord; for his mercies are great: and let me not fall into the hand of man.

15 So the Lord sent a pestilence upon Israel from the morning even to the time appointed: and there died of the people from Dan even to Beersheba seventy thousand men.

16 And when the angel stretched out his hand upon Jerusalem to destroy it, the Lord repented him of the evil, and said to the angel that destroyed the people, It is enough: stay now thine hand. And the angel of the Lord was by the threshingplace of Araunah the Jebusite.

Prayer:

Almighty God, forgive my wrong doings and keep the pestilence from coming near my dwelling I pray

# HEALINGS FROM THE BOOK OF
1 KINGS

King Solomon's Prayer

1 Kings 8:37-40

37 If there be in the land famine, if there be pestilence, blasting, mildew, locust, or if there be caterpiller; if their enemy besiege them in the land of their cities; whatsoever plague, whatsoever sickness there be;

38 What prayer and supplication soever be made by any man, or by all thy people Israel, which shall know every man the plague of his own heart, and spread forth his hands toward this house:

39 Then hear thou in heaven thy dwelling place, and forgive, and do, and give to every man according to his ways, whose heart thou knowest; (for thou, even thou only, knowest the hearts of all the children of men;)

40 That they may fear thee all the days that they live in the land which thou gavest unto our fathers.

Prayer:

Dear Lord in heaven, hear my prayer and forgive, and do and grant to me health according to your grace

1 Kings 13:4-6 — *Jeroboam And The Alter*

4 And it came to pass, when king Jeroboam heard the saying of the man of God, which had cried against the altar in Bethel, that he put forth his hand from the altar, saying, Lay hold on him. And his hand, which he put forth against him, dried up, so that he could not pull it in again to him.

5 The altar also was rent, and the ashes poured out from the altar, according to the sign which the man of God had given by the word of the Lord.

6 And the king answered and said unto the man of God, Intreat now the face of the Lord thy God, and pray for me, that my hand may be restored me again. And the man of God besought the Lord, and the king's hand was restored him again, and became as it was before.

Prayer:

Father forgive me where I have not loved my neighbour as you commanded, and in your mercy restore my health

Elijah And The Woman — 1 Kings 17:17-22

17 And it came to pass after these things, that the son of the woman, the mistress of the house, fell sick; and his sickness was so sore, that there was no breath left in him.

18 And she said unto Elijah, What have I to do with thee, O thou man of God? art thou come unto me to call my sin to remembrance, and to slay my son?

19 And he said unto her, Give me thy son. And he took him out of her bosom, and carried him up into a loft, where he abode, and laid him upon his own bed.

20 And he cried unto the Lord, and said, O Lord my God, hast thou also brought evil upon the widow with whom I sojourn, by slaying her son?

21 And he stretched himself upon the child three times, and cried unto the Lord, and said, O Lord my God, I pray thee, let this child's soul come into him again.

22 And the Lord heard the voice of Elijah; and the soul of the child came into him again, and he revived.

contd.

1 Kings 17:23-24 — *Elijah And The Woman*

23 And Elijah took the child, and brought him down out of the chamber into the house, and delivered him unto his mother: and Elijah said, See, thy son liveth.

24 And the woman said to Elijah, Now by this I know that thou art a man of God, and that the word of the Lord in thy mouth is truth.

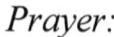

Prayer:

Lord in agreement with the prayers of my Church leaders and elders, I receive healing from all my afflictions

… HEALINGS FROM THE BOOK OF

2 KINGS

God And Elisha   2 Kings 2:14-19

14 And he took the mantle of Elijah that fell from him, and smote the waters, and said, Where is the Lord God of Elijah? and when he also had smitten the waters, they parted hither and thither: and Elisha went over.

15 And when the sons of the prophets which were to view at Jericho saw him, they said, The spirit of Elijah doth rest on Elisha. And they came to meet him, and bowed themselves to the ground before him.

16 And they said unto him, Behold now, there be with thy servants fifty strong men; let them go, we pray thee, and seek thy master: lest peradventure the Spirit of the Lord hath taken him up, and cast him upon some mountain, or into some valley. And he said, Ye shall not send.

17 And when they urged him till he was ashamed, he said, Send. They sent therefore fifty men; and they sought three days, but found him not.

18 And when they came again to him, (for he tarried at Jericho,) he said unto them, Did I not say unto you, Go not?

19 And the men of the city said unto Elisha, Behold, I pray thee, the situation of this city is pleasant, as my lord seeth: but the water is naught, and the ground barren.

contd.

2 Kings 2:20-21   *Jeroboam And The Alter*

20 And he said, Bring me a new cruse, and put salt therein. And they brought it to him.

21 And he went forth unto the spring of the waters, and cast the salt in there, and said, Thus saith the Lord, I have healed these waters; there shall not be from thence any more death or barren land.

Prayer:

Dear God as you healed the spring of the waters, I receive healing for my body from my head to my feet

Elisha And The Shunammite — 2 Kings 4:19-26

19 And he said unto his father, My head, my head. And he said to a lad, Carry him to his mother.

20 And when he had taken him, and brought him to his mother, he sat on her knees till noon, and then died.

21 And she went up, and laid him on the bed of the man of God, and shut the door upon him, and went out.

22 And she called unto her husband, and said, Send me, I pray thee, one of the young men, and one of the asses, that I may run to the man of God, and come again.

23 And he said, Wherefore wilt thou go to him today? it is neither new moon, nor sabbath. And she said, It shall be well.

24 Then she saddled an ass, and said to her servant, Drive, and go forward; slack not thy riding for me, except I bid thee.

25 So she went and came unto the man of God to mount Carmel. And it came to pass, when the man of God saw her afar off, that he said to Gehazi his servant, Behold, yonder is that Shunammite:

26 Run now, I pray thee, to meet her, and say unto her, Is it well with thee? is it well with thy husband? is it well with the child? And she answered, It is well:

contd.

2 Kings 4:27-33

27 And when she came to the man of God to the hill, she caught him by the feet: but Gehazi came near to thrust her away. And the man of God said, Let her alone; for her soul is vexed within her: and the Lord hath hid it from me, and hath not told me.

28 Then she said, Did I desire a son of my lord? did I not say, Do not deceive me?

29 Then he said to Gehazi, Gird up thy loins, and take my staff in thine hand, and go thy way: if thou meet any man, salute him not; and if any salute thee, answer him not again: and lay my staff upon the face of the child.

30 And the mother of the child said, As the Lord liveth, and as thy soul liveth, I will not leave thee. And he arose, and followed her.

31 And Gehazi passed on before them, and laid the staff upon the face of the child; but there was neither voice, nor hearing. Wherefore he went again to meet him, and told him, saying, The child is not awaked.

32 And when Elisha was come into the house, behold, the child was dead, and laid upon his bed.

33 He went in therefore, and shut the door upon them twain, and prayed unto the Lord.

contd.

Elisha And The Shunammite — 2 Kings 4:34-37

34 And he went up, and lay upon the child, and put his mouth upon his mouth, and his eyes upon his eyes, and his hands upon his hands: and stretched himself upon the child; and the flesh of the child waxed warm.

35 Then he returned, and walked in the house to and fro; and went up, and stretched himself upon him: and the child sneezed. seven times, and the child opened his eyes

36 And he called Gehazi, and said, Call this Shunammite. So he called her. And when she was come in unto him, he said, Take up thy son.

37 Then she went in, and fell at his feet, and bowed herself to the ground, and took up her son, and went out.

contd.

Prayer:

*O God of Abraham Isaac and Jacob
who raised the Shunammite woman's child,
raise my loved one I pray*

2 Kings 4:38-41 — *Elisha And The Pottage*

38 And Elisha came again to Gilgal: and there was a dearth in the land; and the sons of the prophets were sitting before him: and he said unto his servant, Set on the great pot, and seethe pottage for the sons of the prophets.

39 And one went out into the field to gather herbs, and found a wild vine, and gathered thereof wild gourds his lap full, and came and shred them into the pot of pottage: for they knew them not.

40 So they poured out for the men to eat. And it came to pass, as they were eating of the pottage, that they cried out, and said, O thou man of God, there is death in the pot. And they could not eat thereof.

41 But he said, Then bring meal. And he cast it into the pot; and he said, Pour out for the people, that they may eat. And there was no harm in the pot.

Prayer:

Dear Lord, according to your power and great mercy I receive healing from food poisoning

Elisha And Naaman

2 Kings 5:6-11

6 And he brought the letter to the king of Israel, saying, Now when this letter is come unto thee, behold, I have therewith sent Naaman my servant to thee, that thou mayest recover him of his leprosy.

7 And it came to pass, when the king of Israel had read the letter, that he rent his clothes, and said, Am I God, to kill and to make alive, that this man doth send unto me to recover a man of his leprosy? wherefore consider, I pray you, and see how he seeketh a quarrel against me.

8 And it was so, when Elisha the man of God had heard that the king of Israel had rent his clothes, that he sent to the king, saying, Wherefore hast thou rent thy clothes? let him come now to me, and he shall know that there is a prophet in Israel.

9 So Naaman came with his horses and with his chariot, and stood at the door of the house of Elisha.

10 And Elisha sent a messenger unto him, saying, Go and wash in Jordan seven times, and thy flesh shall come again to thee, and thou shalt be clean.

11 But Naaman was wroth, and went away, and said, Behold, I thought, He will surely come out to me, and stand, and call on the name of the Lord his God, and strike his hand over the place, and recover the leper.

contd.

Elisha And Naaman — 2 Kings 5:12-14

12 Are not Abana and Pharpar, rivers of Damascus, better than all the waters of Israel? may I not wash in them, and be clean? So he turned and went away in a rage.

13 And his servants came near, and spake unto him, and said, My father, if the prophet had bid thee do some great thing, wouldest thou not have done it? how much rather then, when he saith to thee, Wash, and be clean?

14 Then went he down, and dipped himself seven times in Jordan, according to the saying of the man of God: and his flesh came again like unto the flesh of a little child, and he was clean.

Prayer:

Lord help me to be obedient to your instruction so that I can receive the healing you have already provided

2 Kings 13:18-21

Elisha's Bones

18 And he said, Take the arrows. And he took them. And he said unto the king of Israel, Smite upon the ground. And he smote thrice, and stayed.

19 And the man of God was wroth with him, and said, Thou shouldest have smitten five or six times; then hadst thou smitten Syria till thou hadst consumed it: whereas now thou shalt smite Syria but thrice.

20 And Elisha died, and they buried him. And the bands of the Moabites invaded the land at the coming in of the year.

21 And it came to pass, as they were burying a man, that, behold, they spied a band of men; and they cast the man into the sepulchre of Elisha: and when the man was let down, and touched the bones of Elisha, he revived, and stood up on his feet.

Prayer:

O Lord my God help me persist in your word so that through your revelation my flesh will revive healed

Hezekiah And Isaiah — 2 Kings 20:1-5

1 In those days was Hezekiah sick unto death. And the prophet Isaiah the son of Amoz came to him, and said unto him, Thus saith the Lord, Set thine house in order; for thou shalt die, and not live.

2 Then he turned his face to the wall, and prayed unto the Lord, saying,

3 I beseech thee, O Lord, remember now how I have walked before thee in truth and with a perfect heart, and have done that which is good in thy sight. And Hezekiah wept sore.

4 And it came to pass, afore Isaiah was gone out into the middle court, that the word of the Lord came to him, saying,

5 Turn again, and tell Hezekiah the captain of my people, Thus saith the Lord, the God of David thy father, I have heard thy prayer, I have seen thy tears: behold, I will heal thee: on the third day thou shalt go up unto the house of the Lord.

Prayer:

Almighty God thank you for having mercy on me in Christ Jesus and healing me for I will live and not die

HEALINGS FROM THE BOOK OF
1 CHRONICLES

David's Thanks — 1 Chronicles 16:7-12

7 Then on that day David delivered first this psalm to thank the Lord into the hand of Asaph and his brethren.

8 Give thanks unto the Lord, call upon his name, make known his deeds among the people.

9 Sing unto him, sing psalms unto him, talk ye of all his wondrous works.

10 Glory ye in his holy name: let the heart of them rejoice that seek the Lord.

11 Seek the Lord and his strength, seek his face continually.

12 Remember his marvellous works that he hath done, his wonders, and the judgments of his mouth;

Prayer:

Thank you Lord for your marvellous works, your wonders, for you heal my diseases and make me whole

1 Chronicles 29:25-28 — *David's Good Old Age*

25 And the Lord magnified Solomon exceedingly in the sight of all Israel, and bestowed upon him such royal majesty as had not been on any king before him in Israel.

26 Thus David the son of Jesse reigned over all Israel.

27 And the time that he reigned over Israel was forty years; seven years reigned he in Hebron, and thirty and three years reigned he in Jerusalem.

28 And he died in a good old age, full of days, riches, and honour: and Solomon his son reigned in his stead.

Prayer:

God of glory I receive healing from you to live to a good old age, full of days, riches, and honour

HEALINGS FROM THE BOOK OF
2 CHRONICLES

God And Solomon — 2 Chronicles 7:11-14

11 Thus Solomon finished the house of the Lord, and the king's house: and all that came into Solomon's heart to make in the house of the Lord, and in his own house, he prosperously effected.

12 And the Lord appeared to Solomon by night, and said unto him, I have heard thy prayer, and have chosen this place to myself for an house of sacrifice.

13 If I shut up heaven that there be no rain, or if I command the locusts to devour the land, or if I send pestilence among my people;

14 If my people, which are called by my name, shall humble themselves, and pray, and seek my face, and turn from their wicked ways; then will I hear from heaven, and will forgive their sin, and will heal their land.

Prayer:

O Lord I humble myself, to pray, and seek your face; teach me Lord on how to receive healing for my body

2 Chronicles 30:17-20 — *Hezekiah And The People*

17 For there were many in the congregation that were not sanctified: therefore the Levites had the charge of the killing of the passovers for every one that was not clean, to sanctify them unto the Lord.

18 For a multitude of the people, even many of Ephraim, and Manasseh, Issachar, and Zebulun, had not cleansed themselves, yet did they eat the passover otherwise than it was written. But Hezekiah prayed for them, saying, The good Lord pardon every one

19 That prepareth his heart to seek God, the Lord God of his fathers, though he be not cleansed according to the purification of the sanctuary.

20 And the Lord hearkened to Hezekiah, and healed the people.

Prayer:

As you listened to Hezekiah O Lord, listen to the prayers of the elders and church leaders and heal your people

HEALINGS FROM THE BOOK OF
EZRA

God Is Upon Them For Good — Ezra 8:21-22

21 Then I proclaimed a fast there, at the river of Ahava, that we might afflict ourselves before our God, to seek of him a right way for us, and for our little ones, and for all our substance.

22 For I was ashamed to require of the king a band of soldiers and horsemen to help us against the enemy in the way: because we had spoken unto the king, saying, The hand of our God is upon all them for good that seek him; but his power and his wrath is against all them that forsake him.

Prayer:

Your hand O God is upon all them for good that seek you; as I seek you, may your healing hand rest on me

Ezra 9:8-9 *The Children Of Israel*

8 And now for a little space grace hath been shewed from the Lord our God, to leave us a remnant to escape, and to give us a nail in his holy place, that our God may lighten our eyes, and give us a little reviving in our bondage.

9 For we were bondmen; yet our God hath not forsaken us in our bondage, but hath extended mercy unto us in the sight of the kings of Persia, to give us a reviving, to set up the house of our God, and to repair the desolations thereof, and to give us a wall in Judah and in Jerusalem.

Prayer:

Thank you Father for extending your mercy and reviving me in my bondage, I receive the liberty of healing

HEALINGS FROM THE BOOK OF
NEHEMIAH

The Children Of Israel — Nehemiah 9:19-21

19 Yet thou in thy manifold mercies forsookest them not in the wilderness: the pillar of the cloud departed not from them by day, to lead them in the way; neither the pillar of fire by night, to shew them light, and the way wherein they should go.

20 Thou gavest also thy good spirit to instruct them, and withheldest not thy manna from their mouth, and gavest them water for their thirst

21 Yea, forty years didst thou sustain them in the wilderness, so that they lacked nothing; their clothes waxed not old, and their feet swelled not.

Prayer:

O God who sustained the children of Israel, I receive your sustenance in the healing of my body from sickness

Nehemiah 9:14-15 — *Possess The Land*

14 And madest known unto them thy holy sabbath, and commandedst them precepts, statutes, and laws, by the hand of Moses thy servant:

15 And gavest them bread from heaven for their hunger, and broughtest forth water for them out of the rock for their thirst, and promisedst them that they should go in to possess the land which thou hadst sworn to give them.

Prayer:

I possess the land which you have given me O Lord; and I thank you for in that land is healing and prosperity

HEALINGS FROM THE BOOK OF
ESTHER

Deliverance Arise To The Jews — Esther 4:13-14a

13 Then Mordecai commanded to answer Esther, Think not with thyself that thou shalt escape in the king's house, more than all the Jews.

14 For if thou altogether holdest thy peace at this time, then shall there enlargement and deliverance arise to the Jews from another place;

Prayer:

I will not hold my peace O God but will declare your mighty deliverance from the afflictions of Satan

Esther 9:20-22 — *Esther And Mordecai*

20 And Mordecai wrote these things, and sent letters unto all the Jews that were in all the provinces of the king Ahasuerus, both nigh and far,

21 To stablish this among them, that they should keep the fourteenth day of the month Adar, and the fifteenth day of the same, yearly,

22 As the days wherein the Jews rested from their enemies, and the month which was turned unto them from sorrow to joy, and from mourning into a good day: that they should make them days of feasting and joy, and of sending portions one to another, and gifts to the poor.

Prayer:

I believe I receive healing for my body dear Lord, turning my sorrow to joy, mourning into a good day

HEALINGS FROM THE BOOK OF
JOB

Job And God — Job 5:14-18

14 They meet with darkness in the day time, and grope in the noonday as in the night.

15 But he saveth the poor from the sword, from their mouth, and from the hand of the mighty.

16 So the poor hath hope, and iniquity stoppeth her mouth.

17 Behold, happy is the man whom God correcteth: therefore despise not thou the chastening of the Almighty:

18 For he maketh sore, and bindeth up: he woundeth, and his hands make whole.

Prayer:

O merciful Lord, in your correction, you wounded and made sore, in your mercy heal me and make me whole

Job 33:22-26 — *Job And God*

22 Yea, his soul draweth near unto the grave, and his life to the destroyers.

23 If there be a messenger with him, an interpreter, one among a thousand, to shew unto man his uprightness:

24 Then he is gracious unto him, and saith, Deliver him from going down to the pit: I have found a ransom

25 His flesh shall be fresher than a child's: he shall return to the days of his youth:

26 He shall pray unto God, and he will be favourable unto him: and he shall see his face with joy: for he will render unto man his righteousness.

Prayer

I pray to you O God, be favourable to me, deliver me, heal me that my flesh shall be fresher than a child's

Job And His Friends — Job 36:12-15

12 But if they obey not, they shall perish by the sword, and they shall die without knowledge.

13 But the hypocrites in heart heap up wrath: they cry not when he bindeth them.

14 They die in youth, and their life is among the unclean.

15 He delivereth the poor in his affliction, and openeth their ears in oppression.

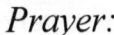

Prayer:

Dear Father, where I have not obeyed you, I repent and ask for forgiveness; deliver me in my affliction I pray

Job 42:7-10 — Job And His Friends

7 And it was so, that after the Lord had spoken these words unto Job, the Lord said to Eliphaz the Temanite, My wrath is kindled against thee, and against thy two friends: for ye have not spoken of me the thing that is right, as my servant Job hath.

8 Therefore take unto you now seven bullocks and seven rams, and go to my servant Job, and offer up for yourselves a burnt offering; and my servant Job shall pray for you: for him will I accept: lest I deal with you after your folly, in that ye have not spoken of me the thing which is right, like my servant Job.

9 So Eliphaz the Temanite and Bildad the Shuhite and Zophar the Naamathite went, and did according as the Lord commanded them: the Lord also accepted Job.

10 And the Lord turned the captivity of Job, when he prayed for his friends: also the Lord gave Job twice as much as he had before.

Prayer:

I receive grace to pray for my friends and love my enemies; as I do so I receive healing from my captivity

HEALINGS FROM THE BOOK OF
PSALMS

God Heard My Prayer — Psalm 6:1-9

1 O Lord, rebuke me not in thine anger, neither chasten me in thy hot displeasure.

2 Have mercy upon me, O Lord; for I am weak: O Lord, heal me; for my bones are vexed.

3 My soul is also sore vexed: but thou, O Lord, how long?

4 Return, O Lord, deliver my soul: oh save me for thy mercies' sake.

5 For in death there is no remembrance of thee: in the grave who shall give thee thanks?

6 I am weary with my groaning; all the night make I my bed to swim; I water my couch with my tears.

7 Mine eye is consumed because of grief; it waxeth old because of all mine enemies.

8 Depart from me, all ye workers of iniquity; for the Lord hath heard the voice of my weeping.

9 The Lord hath heard my supplication; the Lord will receive my prayer.

Prayer:

Lord, deliver me and save me for thy mercies' sake; I thank you and claim my healing which you freely give

Psalm 30:1-4   *David Cried God Healed*

1 I will extol thee, O Lord; for thou hast lifted me up, and hast not made my foes to rejoice over me.

2 O Lord my God, I cried unto thee, and thou hast healed me.

3 O Lord, thou hast brought up my soul from the grave: thou hast kept me alive, that I should not go down to the pit.

4 Sing unto the Lord, O ye saints of his, and give thanks at the remembrance of his holiness.

Prayer:

O Lord my God, I cried unto thee, and thou hast healed me; I give thanks at the remembrance of your holiness

The Lords Mercy To Us   Psalm 41:1-10

1 Blessed is he that considereth the poor: the Lord will deliver him in time of trouble.

2 The Lord will preserve him, and keep him alive; and he shall be blessed upon the earth: and thou wilt not deliver him unto the will of his enemies.

3 The Lord will strengthen him upon the bed of languishing: thou wilt make all his bed in his sickness.

4 I said, Lord, be merciful unto me: heal my soul; for I have sinned against thee.

5 Mine enemies speak evil of me, When shall he die, and his name perish?

6 And if he come to see me, he speaketh vanity: his heart gathereth iniquity to itself; when he goeth abroad, he telleth it.

7 All that hate me whisper together against me: against me do they devise my hurt.

8 An evil disease, say they, cleaveth fast unto him: and now that he lieth he shall rise up no more.

9 Yea, mine own familiar friend, in whom I trusted, which did eat of my bread, hath lifted up his heel against me.

10 But thou, O Lord, be merciful unto me, and raise me up, that I may requite them.

contd.

Psalm 41:11-13   *The Lords Mercy To Us*

11 By this I know that thou favourest me, because mine enemy doth not triumph over me.

12 And as for me, thou upholdest me in mine integrity, and settest me before thy face for ever.

13 Blessed be the Lord God of Israel from everlasting, and to everlasting. Amen, and Amen.

Prayer:

O God who upholds me in my integrity, I receive your healing in my body, crushing all the works of the devil

Thy Youth Renewed   Psalm 103:1-5

1 Bless the Lord, O my soul: and all that is within me, bless his holy name.

2 Bless the Lord, O my soul, and forget not all his benefits:

3 Who forgiveth all thine iniquities; who healeth all thy diseases;

4 Who redeemeth thy life from destruction; who crowneth thee with lovingkindness and tender mercies;

5 Who satisfieth thy mouth with good things; so that thy youth is renewed like the eagle's.

Prayer:

I give thanks to you almighty God who forgives all my iniquities, who heals all my diseases

Psalm 103:15-20   *He Sent His Word*

15 Oh that men would praise the Lord for his goodness, and for his wonderful works to the children of men!

16 For he hath broken the gates of brass, and cut the bars of iron in sunder.

17 Fools because of their transgression, and because of their iniquities, are afflicted.

18 Their soul abhorreth all manner of meat; and they draw near unto the gates of death.

19 Then they cry unto the Lord in their trouble, and he saveth them out of their distresses.

20 He sent his word, and healed them, and delivered them from their destructions.

Prayer:

Thank you Lord for you sent your word, and healed me, and delivered me from my destructions

He Healeth The Broken   Psalm 147:1-3

1 Praise ye the Lord: for it is good to sing praises unto our God; for it is pleasant; and praise is comely.

2 The Lord doth build up Jerusalem: he gathereth together the outcasts of Israel.

3 He healeth the broken in heart, and bindeth up their wounds.

Prayer:

O Lord who heals the broken in heart and binds up their wounds, I receive healing and binding up of my wounds

HEALINGS FROM THE BOOK OF
PROVERBS

God's Word And Health — Proverbs 3:1-8

1 My son, forget not my law; but let thine heart keep my commandments:

2 For length of days, and long life, and peace, shall they add to thee.

3 Let not mercy and truth forsake thee: bind them about thy neck; write them upon the table of thine heart:

4 So shalt thou find favour and good understanding in the sight of God and man.

5 Trust in the Lord with all thine heart; and lean not unto thine own understanding.

6 In all thy ways acknowledge him, and he shall direct thy paths.

7 Be not wise in thine own eyes: fear the Lord, and depart from evil.

8 It shall be health to thy navel, and marrow to thy bones.

Prayer:

Lord, grant me grace to follow Your commandments, bringing long life, health, and strength to my bones

Proverbs 4:20-22 *God's Word And Health*

20 My son, attend to my words; incline thine ear unto my sayings.

21 Let them not depart from thine eyes; keep them in the midst of thine heart.

22 For they are life unto those that find them, and health to all their flesh.

Prayer:

Father I will incline mine ear unto your word; as I do this, I receive life and health to all my flesh

Man's Word And Health **Proverbs 12:15-18**

15 The way of a fool is right in his own eyes: but he that hearkeneth unto counsel is wise.

16 A fool's wrath is presently known: but a prudent man covereth shame.

17 He that speaketh truth sheweth forth righteousness: but a false witness deceit.

18 There is that speaketh like the piercings of a sword: but the tongue of the wise is health.

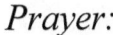

Prayer:

May my tongue O Lord not be the piercings of a sword but rather the tongue of the wise bringing health to all

Proverbs 13:14-17 — *Faithful And Health*

14 The law of the wise is a fountain of life, to depart from the snares of death.

15 Good understanding giveth favour: but the way of transgressors is hard.

16 Every prudent man dealeth with knowledge: but a fool layeth open his folly.

17 A wicked messenger falleth into mischief: but a faithful ambassador is health.

Prayer:

Father, grant me wisdom to depart from the snares of death and to attract enjoy health

Sound Heart Life Of The Flesh   Proverbs 14:26-30

26 In the fear of the Lord is strong confidence: and his children shall have a place of refuge.

27 The fear of the Lord is a fountain of life, to depart from the snares of death.

28 In the multitude of people is the king's honour: but in the want of people is the destruction of the prince.

29 He that is slow to wrath is of great understanding: but he that is hasty of spirit exalteth folly.

30 A sound heart is the life of the flesh: but envy the rottenness of the bones.

Prayer:

Lord, where envying has brought rottenness to my bones, please forgive; I receive a sound heart - life to my flesh

Proverbs 15:26-30 — *A Good Report*

26 The thoughts of the wicked are an abomination to the Lord: but the words of the pure are pleasant words.

27 He that is greedy of gain troubleth his own house; but he that hateth gifts shall live.

28 The heart of the righteous studieth to answer: but the mouth of the wicked poureth out evil things.

29 The Lord is far from the wicked: but he heareth the prayer of the righteous.

30 The light of the eyes rejoiceth the heart: and a good report maketh the bones fat.

Prayer:

Hear my prayer O Lord and grant me a good report so that my bones will be fat with healing and health

Pleasant Words And Health Proverbs 16:21-24

21 The wise in heart shall be called prudent: and the sweetness of the lips increaseth learning.

22 Understanding is a wellspring of life unto him that hath it: but the instruction of fools is folly.

23 The heart of the wise teacheth his mouth, and addeth learning to his lips.

24 Pleasant words are as an honeycomb, sweet to the soul, and health to the bones.

Prayer:

Lord I receive grace to speak pleasant words to myself and others, sweet to the soul, and health to our bones

Proverbs 17:19-22

Merry Heart Medicine

19 He loveth transgression that loveth strife: and he that exalteth his gate seeketh destruction.

20 He that hath a froward heart findeth no good: and he that hath a perverse tongue falleth into mischief.

21 He that begetteth a fool doeth it to his sorrow: and the father of a fool hath no joy.

22 A merry heart doeth good like a medicine: but a broken spirit drieth the bones.

Prayer:

O Lord my God, help me build a merry heart through your word that I may enjoy its good medicine in my flesh

HEALINGS FROM THE BOOK OF
ECCLESIASTES

Time To Heal
Ecclesiastes 3:1-3

1. To every thing there is a season, and a time to every purpose under the heaven:

2 A time to be born, and a time to die; a time to plant, and a time to pluck up that which is planted;

3 A time to kill, and a time to heal; a time to break down, and a time to build up;

Prayer:

It's my time to heal so Lord I claim and hold fast to my healing in Christ Jesus

Ecclesiastes 11:9-10a   *Put Away Evil From Flesh*

9 Rejoice, O young man, in thy youth; and let thy heart cheer thee in the days of thy youth, and walk in the ways of thine heart, and in the sight of thine eyes: but know thou, that for all these things God will bring thee into judgment.

10 Therefore remove sorrow from thy heart, and put away evil from thy flesh:

Prayer:

I receive grace O Lord to remove sorrow from my heart and put away sickness, diseases and pain from my flesh

HEALINGS FROM THE BOOK OF

SONG OF SOLOMON

Time Of Singing — **Song of Solomon 2:10-12**

10 My beloved spake, and said unto me, Rise up, my love, my fair one, and come away.

11 For, lo, the winter is past, the rain is over and gone;

12 The flowers appear on the earth; the time of the singing of birds is come, and the voice of the turtle is heard in our land;

Prayer:

Lord thank you for as flowers appear on the earth; the time of the singing of birds is come, so is my healing

Song of Solomon 4:13-15   *Well Of Living Waters*

13 Thy plants are an orchard of pomegranates, with pleasant fruits; camphire, with spikenard,

14 Spikenard and saffron; calamus and cinnamon, with all trees of frankincense; myrrh and aloes, with all the chief spices:

15 A fountain of gardens, a well of living waters, and streams from Lebanon.

Prayer:

Lord your plants are a fountain of gardens, a well of living waters from which I draw my healing

HEALINGS FROM THE BOOK OF
ISAIAH

The Children Of Israel — Isaiah 40:26-29

26 Lift up your eyes on high, and behold who hath created these things, that bringeth out their host by number: he calleth them all by names by the greatness of his might, for that he is strong in power; not one faileth.

27 Why sayest thou, O Jacob, and speakest, O Israel, My way is hid from the Lord, and my judgment is passed over from my God?

28 Hast thou not known? hast thou not heard, that the everlasting God, the Lord, the Creator of the ends of the earth, fainteth not, neither is weary? there is no searching of his understanding.

29 He giveth power to the faint; and to them that have no might he increaseth strength.

Prayer:

O God who does not faint, nor is weary but gives power to the faint, I pray that you strengthen and heal me

Isaiah 41:8-10   *The Children Of Israel*

8 But thou, Israel, art my servant, Jacob whom I have chosen, the seed of Abraham my friend.

9 Thou whom I have taken from the ends of the earth, and called thee from the chief men thereof, and said unto thee, Thou art my servant; I have chosen thee, and not cast thee away.

10 Fear thou not; for I am with thee: be not dismayed; for I am thy God: I will strengthen thee; yea, I will help thee; yea, I will uphold thee with the right hand of my righteousness.

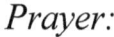

Prayer:

Lord I will not fear, for you are my God who strengthens me, helps and upholds me unto health and prosperity

The Children Of Israel — Isaiah 19:19-22

19 In that day shall there be an altar to the Lord in the midst of the land of Egypt, and a pillar at the border thereof to the Lord.

20 And it shall be for a sign and for a witness unto the Lord of hosts in the land of Egypt: for they shall cry unto the Lord because of the oppressors, and he shall send them a saviour, and a great one, and he shall deliver them.

21 And the Lord shall be known to Egypt, and the Egyptians shall know the Lord in that day, and shall do sacrifice and oblation; yea, they shall vow a vow unto the Lord, and perform it.

22 And the Lord shall smite Egypt: he shall smite and heal it: and they shall return even to the Lord, and he shall be intreated of them, and shall heal them.

Prayer:

Thank you Lord for sending a saviour Jesus Christ through whom you heal all; I receive my healing

Isaiah 30:23-26   *The Children Of Israel*

23 Then shall he give the rain of thy seed, that thou shalt sow the ground withal; and bread of the increase of the earth, and it shall be fat and plenteous: in that day shall thy cattle feed in large pastures.

24 The oxen likewise and the young asses that ear the ground shall eat clean provender, which hath been winnowed with the shovel and with the fan

25 And there shall be upon every high mountain, and upon every high hill, rivers and streams of waters in the day of the great slaughter, when the towers fall.

26 Moreover the light of the moon shall be as the light of the sun, and the light of the sun shall be sevenfold, as the light of seven days, in the day that the Lord bindeth up the breach of his people, and healeth the stroke of their wound.

Prayer:

Great God you have blessed your people with fat and plenty; in your mercy I also claim healing in my body

The Children Of God — Isaiah 53:1-5

1 Who hath believed our report? and to whom is the arm of the Lord revealed?

2 For he shall grow up before him as a tender plant, and as a root out of a dry ground: he hath no form nor comeliness; and when we shall see him, there is no beauty that we should desire him.

3 He is despised and rejected of men; a man of sorrows, and acquainted with grief: and we hid as it were our faces from him; he was despised, and we esteemed him not.

4 Surely he hath borne our griefs, and carried our sorrows: yet we did esteem him stricken, smitten of God, and afflicted.

5 But he was wounded for our transgressions, he was bruised for our iniquities: the chastisement of our peace was upon him; and with his stripes we are healed.

Prayer:

Father, you say that with the stripes of Jesus I am healed so I thank you because you already healed me!

Isaiah 57:15-19

The Children Of God

15 For thus saith the high and lofty One that inhabiteth eternity, whose name is Holy; I dwell in the high and holy place, with him also that is of a contrite and humble spirit, to revive the spirit of the humble, and to revive the heart of the contrite ones.

16 For I will not contend for ever, neither will I be always wroth: for the spirit should fail before me, and the souls which I have made.

17 For the iniquity of his covetousness was I wroth, and smote him: I hid me, and was wroth, and he went on frowardly in the way of his heart.

18 I have seen his ways, and will heal him: I will lead him also, and restore comforts unto him and to his mourners.

19 I create the fruit of the lips; Peace, peace to him that is far off, and to him that is near, saith the Lord; and I will heal him.

Prayer:

O Lord I come to you with a contrite and humble spirit asking for your forgiveness and to receive healing

The Children Of Israel — Isaiah 58:1-6

1 Cry aloud, spare not, lift up thy voice like a trumpet, and shew my people their transgression, and the house of Jacob their sins.

2 Yet they seek me daily, and delight to know my ways, as a nation that did righteousness, and forsook not the ordinance of their God: they ask of me the ordinances of justice; they take delight in approaching to God.

3 Wherefore have we fasted, say they, and thou seest not? wherefore have we afflicted our soul, and thou takest no knowledge? Behold, in the day of your fast ye find pleasure, and exact all your labours.

4 Behold, ye fast for strife and debate, and to smite with the fist of wickedness: ye shall not fast as ye do this day, to make your voice to be heard on high.

5 Is it such a fast that I have chosen? a day for a man to afflict his soul? is it to bow down his head as a bulrush, and to spread sackcloth and ashes under him? wilt thou call this a fast, and an acceptable day to the Lord?

6 Is not this the fast that I have chosen? to loose the bands of wickedness, to undo the heavy burdens, and to let the oppressed go free, and that ye break every yoke?

contd.

Isaiah 58:7-8 *The Children Of Israel*

7 Is it not to deal thy bread to the hungry, and that thou bring the poor that are cast out to thy house? when thou seest the naked, that thou cover him; and that thou hide not thyself from thine own flesh?

8 Then shall thy light break forth as the morning, and thine health shall spring forth speedily: and thy righteousness shall go before thee; the glory of the Lord shall be thy reward.

Prayer:

Father teach me to fast; free me from wickedness, burdens, yokes, and my health shall spring forth speedily

HEALINGS FROM THE BOOK OF
JEREMIAH

Healing Backsliding — Jeremiah 3:19-22

19 But I said, How shall I put thee among the children, and give thee a pleasant land, a goodly heritage of the hosts of nations? and I said, Thou shalt call me, My father; and shalt not turn away from me.

20 Surely as a wife treacherously departeth from her husband, so have ye dealt treacherously with me, O house of Israel, saith the Lord.

21 A voice was heard upon the high places, weeping and supplications of the children of Israel: for they have perverted their way, and they have forgotten the Lord their God.

22 Return, ye backsliding children, and I will heal your backslidings. Behold, we come unto thee; for thou art the Lord our God.

Prayer:

O Merciful Father, I return to you and ask that you forgive my backsliding and heal me

Jeremiah 8:20-22 *God Brings Health And Cure*

20 The harvest is past, the summer is ended, and we are not saved.

21 For the hurt of the daughter of my people am I hurt; I am black; astonishment hath taken hold on me.

22 Is there no balm in Gilead; is there no physician there? why then is not the health of the daughter of my people recovered?

Prayer:

You O Lord are the balm in Gilead and our physician, restore our health we pray

Heal me O Lord — Jeremiah 17:12-14

12 A glorious high throne from the beginning is the place of our sanctuary.

13 O Lord, the hope of Israel, all that forsake thee shall be ashamed, and they that depart from me shall be written in the earth, because they have forsaken the Lord, the fountain of living waters.

14 Heal me, O Lord, and I shall be healed; save me, and I shall be saved: for thou art my praise.

Prayer:

Heal me, O Lord, and I shall be healed; save me, and I shall be saved: for you are my praise

Jeremiah 30:15-17   *God Restores And Heals*

15 Why criest thou for thine affliction? thy sorrow is incurable for the multitude of thine iniquity: because thy sins were increased, I have done these things unto thee.

16 Therefore all they that devour thee shall be devoured; and all thine adversaries, every one of them, shall go into captivity; and they that spoil thee shall be a spoil, and all that prey upon thee will I give for a prey.

17 For I will restore health unto thee, and I will heal thee of thy wounds, saith the Lord; because they called thee an Outcast, saying, This is Zion, whom no man seeketh after.

Prayer:

Thank you God almighty, for I believe you have restored health to me, and healed me of my wound

God Brings Health And Cure — Jeremiah 33:3-6

3 Call unto me, and I will answer thee, and show thee great and mighty things, which thou knowest not.

4 For thus saith the Lord, the God of Israel, concerning the houses of this city, and concerning the houses of the kings of Judah, which are thrown down by the mounts, and by the sword;

5 They come to fight with the Chaldeans, but it is to fill them with the dead bodies of men, whom I have slain in mine anger and in my fury, and for all whose wickedness I have hid my face from this city.

6 Behold, I will bring it health and cure, and I will cure them, and will reveal unto them the abundance of peace and truth.

Prayer:

Father, I Call to you and you answer me bringing health and cure to my body for you said "and I will cure them"

HEALINGS FROM THE BOOK OF
LAMENTATIONS

I Will Hope In God — Lamentations 3:21-24

21 This I recall to my mind, therefore have I hope.

22 It is of the Lord's mercies that we are not consumed, because his compassions fail not.

23 They are new every morning: great is thy faithfulness.

24 The Lord is my portion, saith my soul; therefore will I hope in him.

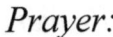

Prayer:

Thank you Lord for healing me; because of your mercies we are not consumed, and your compassions fail not

Lamentations 3:25-33 *God Doth Not Afflict Willingly*

25 The Lord is good unto them that wait for him, to the soul that seeketh him.

26 It is good that a man should both hope and quietly wait for the salvation of the Lord.

27 It is good for a man that he bear the yoke in his youth.

28 He sitteth alone and keepeth silence, because he hath borne it upon him.

29 He putteth his mouth in the dust; if so be there may be hope.

30 He giveth his cheek to him that smiteth him: he is filled full with reproach.

31 For the Lord will not cast off for ever:

32 But though he cause grief, yet will he have compassion according to the multitude of his mercies.

33 For he doth not afflict willingly nor grieve the children of men.

Prayer:

O Lord who does not cast off for ever, have compassion according to the multitude of your mercies and heal me

God Has Redeemed My — Lamentations 3:53-58

53 They have cut off my life in the dungeon, and cast a stone upon me.

54 Waters flowed over mine head; then I said, I am cut off.

55 I called upon thy name, O Lord, out of the low dungeon.

56 Thou hast heard my voice: hide not thine ear at my breathing, at my cry

57 Thou drewest near in the day that I called upon thee: thou saidst, Fear not.

58 O Lord, thou hast pleaded the causes of my soul; thou hast redeemed my life.

Prayer:

I call upon your name O Lord, you have heard my voice: hide not thine ear at my cry, I receive healing from you

Lamentations 5:19-21   *Renew Our Day*

19 Thou, O Lord, remainest for ever; thy throne from generation to generation.

20 Wherefore dost thou forget us for ever, and forsake us so long time?

21 Turn thou us unto thee, O Lord, and we shall be turned; renew our days as of old.

Prayer:

I turn to you O Lord; in your mercy, renew my days as of old in my body and mind

HEALINGS FROM THE BOOK OF
EZEKIEL

Strengthen That Which Was Sick   Ezekiel 34:12-16

12 As a shepherd seeketh out his flock in the day that he is among his sheep that are scattered; so will I seek out my sheep, and will deliver them out of all places where they have been scattered in the cloudy and dark day.

13 And I will bring them out from the people, and gather them from the countries, and will bring them to their own land, and feed them upon the mountains of Israel by the rivers, and in all the inhabited places of the country.

14 I will feed them in a good pasture, and upon the high mountains of Israel shall their fold be: there shall they lie in a good fold, and in a fat pasture shall they feed upon the mountains of Israel.

15 I will feed my flock, and I will cause them to lie down, saith the Lord God.

16 I will seek that which was lost, and bring again that which was driven away, and will bind up that which was broken, and will strengthen that which was sick: but I will destroy the fat and the strong; I will feed them with judgment.

Prayer:

*I receive this promise O God,
that you will bind up that which was broken,
and strengthen that which was sick*

Ezekiel 37:3-9 — *Dry Bones*

3 And he said unto me, Son of man, can these bones live? And I answered, O Lord God, thou knowest.

4 Again he said unto me, Prophesy upon these bones, and say unto them, O ye dry bones, hear the word of the Lord.

5 Thus saith the Lord God unto these bones; Behold, I will cause breath to enter into you, and ye shall live:

6 And I will lay sinews upon you, and will bring up flesh upon you, and cover you with skin, and put breath in you, and ye shall live; and ye shall know that I am the Lord.

7 So I prophesied as I was commanded: and as I prophesied, there was a noise, and behold a shaking, and the bones came together, bone to his bone.

8 And when I beheld, lo, the sinews and the flesh came up upon them, and the skin covered them above: but there was no breath in them.

9 Then said he unto me, Prophesy unto the wind, prophesy, son of man, and say to the wind, Thus saith the Lord God; Come from the four winds, O breath, and breathe upon these slain, that they may live.

contd.

Dry Bones   **Ezekiel 37:10**

10 So I prophesied as he commanded me, and the breath came into them, and they lived, and stood up upon their feet, an exceeding great army.

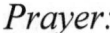

Prayer:

God of Abraham, Isaac and Jacob who made dry bones live, raise to life my loved one as I give the command

Ezekiel 47:6-9

For They Shall Be Healed

6 And he said unto me, Son of man, hast thou seen this? Then he brought me, and caused me to return to the brink of the river.

7 Now when I had returned, behold, at the bank of the river were very many trees on the one side and on the other.

8 Then said he unto me, These waters issue out toward the east country, and go down into the desert, and go into the sea: which being brought forth into the sea, the waters shall be healed.

9 And it shall come to pass, that every thing that liveth, which moveth, whithersoever the rivers shall come, shall live: and there shall be a very great multitude of fish, because these waters shall come thither: for they shall be healed; and every thing shall live whither the river cometh.

Prayer:

As the rivers of living water Jesus flows in me bringing the life of God, I shall live and not die for I am healed

HEALINGS FROM THE BOOK OF
DANIEL

God Hath Sent His Angel — Daniel 6:19-22

19 Then the king arose very early in the morning, and went in haste unto the den of lions.

20 And when he came to the den, he cried with a lamentable voice unto Daniel: and the king spake and said to Daniel, O Daniel, servant of the living God, is thy God, whom thou servest continually, able to deliver thee from the lions?

21 Then said Daniel unto the king, O king, live for ever.

22 My God hath sent his angel, and hath shut the lions' mouths, that they have not hurt me: forasmuch as before him innocency was found in me; and also before thee, O king, have I done no hurt.

Prayer:

Dear God, in my affliction send your angels, and shut the lions' mouths

Daniel 9:17-19 — *Daniels Prayer*

17 Now therefore, O our God, hear the prayer of thy servant, and his supplications, and cause thy face to shine upon thy sanctuary that is desolate, for the Lord's sake.

18 O my God, incline thine ear, and hear; open thine eyes, and behold our desolations, and the city which is called by thy name: for we do not present our supplications before thee for our righteousnesses, but for thy great mercies.

19 O Lord, hear; O Lord, forgive; O Lord, hearken and do; defer not, for thine own sake, O my God: for thy city and thy people are called by thy name.

Prayer:

Thank you for hearing the prayer of your child in your great mercy; I therefore believe I receive my healing

HEALINGS FROM THE BOOK OF
HOSEA

The Latter And Former Rain — Hosea 6:1-3

1 Come, and let us return unto the Lord: for he hath torn, and he will heal us; he hath smitten, and he will bind us up.

2 After two days will he revive us: in the third day he will raise us up, and we shall live in his sight.

3 Then shall we know, if we follow on to know the Lord: his going forth is prepared as the morning; and he shall come unto us as the rain, as the latter and former rain unto the earth.

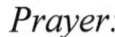

Prayer:

As I return to you merciful Lord, heal me; come to me as the rain, as the latter and former rain unto the earth

Hosea 11:1-4　　　　　　*I Healed Them*

1 When Israel was a child, then I loved him, and called my son out of Egypt.

2 As they called them, so they went from them: they sacrificed unto Baalim, and burned incense to graven images.

3 I taught Ephraim also to go, taking them by their arms; but they knew not that I healed them.

4 I drew them with cords of a man, with bands of love: and I was to them as they that take off the yoke on their jaws, and I laid meat unto them.

Prayer:

Lord I repent of my idolatry and thank you for your kindness and healing which I neglected in the past

I Will Heal Their Backsliding — Hosea 14:1-6

1 O Israel, return unto the Lord thy God; for thou hast fallen by thine iniquity.

2 Take with you words, and turn to the Lord: say unto him, Take away all iniquity, and receive us graciously: so will we render the calves of our lips.

3 Asshur shall not save us; we will not ride upon horses: neither will we say any more to the work of our hands, Ye are our gods: for in thee the fatherless findeth mercy.

4 I will heal their backsliding, I will love them freely: for mine anger is turned away from him.

5 I will be as the dew unto Israel: he shall grow as the lily, and cast forth his roots as Lebanon.

6 His branches shall spread, and his beauty shall be as the olive tree, and his smell as Lebanon.

Prayer:

I come to you O God to thank you for healing my backsliding and granting me blessings and beauty

HEALINGS FROM THE BOOK OF
JOEL

He Is Gracious And Merciful — Joel 2:12-13

12 Therefore also now, saith the Lord, turn ye even to me with all your heart, and with fasting, and with weeping, and with mourning:

13 And rend your heart, and not your garments, and turn unto the Lord your God: for he is gracious and merciful, slow to anger, and of great kindness, and repenteth him of the evil.

Prayer:

Lord, I turn to you with all my heart with fasting, and with weeping, and with mourning; restore and heal me

Joel 3:9-10 *The Weak Say, I Am Strong*

9 Proclaim ye this among the Gentiles; Prepare war, wake up the mighty men, let all the men of war draw near; let them come up:

10 Beat your plowshares into swords and your pruninghooks into spears: let the weak say, I am strong.

Prayer:

In your name O Mighty God I take the battle to the enemy and take my healing, for in Jesus I am strong!

Judah Shall Dwell For Ever — Joel 3:16-20

16 The Lord also shall roar out of Zion, and utter his voice from Jerusalem; and the heavens and the earth shall shake: but the Lord will be the hope of his people, and the strength of the children of Israel.

17 So shall ye know that I am the Lord your God dwelling in Zion, my holy mountain: then shall Jerusalem be holy, and there shall no strangers pass through her any more.

18 And it shall come to pass in that day, that the mountains shall drop down new wine, and the hills shall flow with milk, and all the rivers of Judah shall flow with waters, and a fountain shall come forth out of the house of the Lord, and shall water the valley of Shittim.

19 Egypt shall be a desolation, and Edom shall be a desolate wilderness, for the violence against the children of Judah, because they have shed innocent blood in their land.

20 But Judah shall dwell for ever, and Jerusalem from generation to generation.

Prayer:

Lord you are my hope and strength; I receive your healing in my body as the fountain of waters

HEALINGS FROM THE BOOK OF
AMOS

Seek The Lord, And Live — Amos 5:4-6

4 For thus saith the Lord unto the house of Israel, Seek ye me, and ye shall live:

5 But seek not Bethel, nor enter into Gilgal, and pass not to Beersheba: for Gilgal shall surely go into captivity, and Bethel shall come to nought.

6 Seek the Lord, and ye shall live; lest he break out like fire in the house of Joseph, and devour it, and there be none to quench it in Bethel.

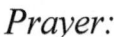

Prayer:

Lord, I turn from my habits of idolatry and seek you that I might live and not be devoured like fire

Amos 9:13-15 — *Restoring Israel's Captivity*

13 Behold, the days come, saith the Lord, that the plowman shall overtake the reaper, and the treader of grapes him that soweth seed; and the mountains shall drop sweet wine, and all the hills shall melt.

14 And I will bring again the captivity of my people of Israel, and they shall build the waste cities, and inhabit them; and they shall plant vineyards, and drink the wine thereof; they shall also make gardens, and eat the fruit of them.

15 And I will plant them upon their land, and they shall no more be pulled up out of their land which I have given them, saith the Lord thy God.

Prayer:

Father, restore my captivity and heal my body; let the waste parts of my body recover and be renewed

HEALINGS FROM THE BOOK OF
OBADIAH

Possess Their Possessions — **Obadiah 1:16-17**

16 For as ye have drunk upon my holy mountain, so shall all the heathen drink continually, yea, they shall drink, and they shall swallow down, and they shall be as though they had not been.

17 But upon mount Zion shall be deliverance, and there shall be holiness; and the house of Jacob shall possess their possessions.

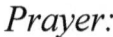

Prayer:

O God, I receive deliverance and embrace holiness as I possess my possessions of healing and prosperity in Jesus

Obadiah 1:19-20 — *Possess Their Possessions*

19 And they of the south shall possess the mount of Esau; and they of the plain the Philistines: and they shall possess the fields of Ephraim, and the fields of Samaria: and Benjamin shall possess Gilead.

20 And the captivity of this host of the children of Israel shall possess that of the Canaanites, even unto Zarephath; and the captivity of Jerusalem, which is in Sepharad, shall possess the cities of the south.

Prayer:

Almighty God, thank you as I possess the fields of prosperity and freedom from the captivity of sickness

HEALINGS FROM THE BOOK OF
JONAH

Jonah Prays — Jonah 2:1-7

1 Then Jonah prayed unto the Lord his God out of the fish's belly,

2 And said, I cried by reason of mine affliction unto the Lord, and he heard me; out of the belly of hell cried I, and thou heardest my voice.

3 For thou hadst cast me into the deep, in the midst of the seas; and the floods compassed me about: all thy billows and thy waves passed over me.

4 Then I said, I am cast out of thy sight; yet I will look again toward thy holy temple.

5 The waters compassed me about, even to the soul: the depth closed me round about, the weeds were wrapped about my head.

6 I went down to the bottoms of the mountains; the earth with her bars was about me for ever: yet hast thou brought up my life from corruption, O Lord my God.

7 When my soul fainted within me I remembered the Lord: and my prayer came in unto thee, into thine holy temple.

contd.

Jonah 2:8-10 — *Jonah Prays*

8 They that observe lying vanities forsake their own mercy.

9 But I will sacrifice unto thee with the voice of thanksgiving; I will pay that that I have vowed. Salvation is of the Lord.

10 And the Lord spake unto the fish, and it vomited out Jonah upon the dry land.

Prayer:

O God of mercy and grace, forgive my disobedience, deliver me from my afflictions and restore my health

Thou Art A Gracious God — Jonah 3:10; 4:1-2

10 And God saw their works, that they turned from their evil way; and God repented of the evil, that he had said that he would do unto them; and he did it not.

1 But it displeased Jonah exceedingly, and he was very angry.

2 And he prayed unto the Lord, and said, I pray thee, O Lord, was not this my saying, when I was yet in my country? Therefore I fled before unto Tarshish: for I knew that thou art a gracious God, and merciful, slow to anger, and of great kindness, and repentest thee of the evil.

Prayer:

Father, you are a gracious God, and merciful, slow to anger and of great kindness, hence I receive my healing

HEALINGS FROM THE BOOK OF
MICAH

Remnant And Strong Nation — Micah 4:6-7

6 In that day, saith the Lord, will I assemble her that halteth, and I will gather her that is driven out, and her that I have afflicted;

7 And I will make her that halted a remnant, and her that was cast far off a strong nation: and the Lord shall reign over them in mount Zion from henceforth, even for ever.

Prayer:

Lord, heal me from my affliction; make me a strong nation as I submit my will to yours

HEALINGS FROM THE BOOK OF NAHUM

Affliction Shall Not Rise Up — Nahum 1:7-9

7 The Lord is good, a strong hold in the day of trouble; and he knoweth them that trust in him.

8 But with an overrunning flood he will make an utter end of the place thereof, and darkness shall pursue his enemies.

9 What do ye imagine against the Lord? he will make an utter end: affliction shall not rise up the second time.

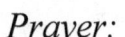

Prayer:

O Lord you are good, a stronghold in the day of trouble; heal me in my affliction and may it not rise again

Nahum 1:12-13 — *I Will Afflict Thee No More*

12 Thus saith the Lord; Though they be quiet, and likewise many, yet thus shall they be cut down, when he shall pass through. Though I have afflicted thee, I will afflict thee no more.

13 For now will I break his yoke from off thee, and will burst thy bonds in sunder.

Prayer:

I command the yoke of the devil in my life broken, and decree that no affliction shall befall me in Jesus name

HEALINGS FROM THE BOOK OF
HABAKKUK

The Lord God Is My Strength   Habakkuk 3:15-19

15 Thou didst walk through the sea with thine horses, through the heap of great waters.

16 When I heard, my belly trembled; my lips quivered at the voice: rottenness entered into my bones, and I trembled in myself, that I might rest in the day of trouble: when he cometh up unto the people, he will invade them with his troops.

17 Although the fig tree shall not blossom, neither shall fruit be in the vines; the labour of the olive shall fail, and the fields shall yield no meat; the flock shall be cut off from the fold, and there shall be no herd in the stalls:

18 Yet I will rejoice in the Lord, I will joy in the God of my salvation.

19 The Lord God is my strength, and he will make my feet like hinds' feet, and he will make me to walk upon mine high places. To the chief singer on my stringed instruments.

Prayer:

Father, though the fig tree shall not blossom, I believe the command of Jesus; the root is dead and I am healed

HEALINGS FROM THE BOOK OF
ZEPHANIAH

Lord Their God Shall Visit — Zephaniah 2:6-7

6 And the sea coast shall be dwellings and cottages for shepherds, and folds for flocks.

7 And the coast shall be for the remnant of the house of Judah; they shall feed thereupon: in the houses of Ashkelon shall they lie down in the evening: for the Lord their God shall visit them, and turn away their captivity.

Prayer:

Dear Lord, visit me according to your word and turn away my captivity of sickness and disease

HEALINGS FROM THE BOOK OF
HAGGAI

In This Place Will I Give Peace — **Haggai 2:6-9**

6 For thus saith the Lord of hosts; Yet once, it is a little while, and I will shake the heavens, and the earth, and the sea, and the dry land;

7 And I will shake all nations, and the desire of all nations shall come: and I will fill this house with glory, saith the Lord of hosts.

8 The silver is mine, and the gold is mine, saith the Lord of hosts.

9 The glory of this latter house shall be greater than of the former, saith the Lord of hosts: and in this place will I give peace, saith the Lord of hosts.

Prayer:

O God I receive your peace in my body as your glory fills and heals your temple which is my body

HEALINGS FROM THE BOOK OF
ZECHARIAH

Thou Shalt Become A Plain — Zechariah 4:6-7

6 Then he answered and spake unto me, saying, This is the word of the Lord unto Zerubbabel, saying, Not by might, nor by power, but by my spirit, saith the Lord of hosts.

7 Who art thou, O great mountain? before Zerubbabel thou shalt become a plain: and he shall bring forth the headstone thereof with shoutings, crying, Grace, grace unto it.

Prayer:

O mountain of sickness and disease in my body, I command you in Jesus name to become a plain

Zechariah 8:12-13   *So Will I Save You*

12 For the seed shall be prosperous; the vine shall give her fruit, and the ground shall give her increase, and the heavens shall give their dew; and I will cause the remnant of this people to possess all these things.

13 And it shall come to pass, that as ye were a curse among the heathen, O house of Judah, and house of Israel; so will I save you, and ye shall be a blessing: fear not, but let your hands be strong.

Prayer:

Thank you Jesus, for redeeming me from the curse; I therefore believe I receive my healing you have paid for

I Will Render Double Unto Thee   Zechariah 9:9-12

9 Rejoice greatly, O daughter of Zion; shout, O daughter of Jerusalem: behold, thy King cometh unto thee: he is just, and having salvation; lowly, and riding upon an ass, and upon a colt the foal of an ass.

10 And I will cut off the chariot from Ephraim, and the horse from Jerusalem, and the battle bow shall be cut off: and he shall speak peace unto the heathen: and his dominion shall be from sea even to sea, and from the river even to the ends of the earth.

11 As for thee also, by the blood of thy covenant I have sent forth thy prisoners out of the pit wherein is no water.

12 Turn you to the strong hold, ye prisoners of hope: even to day do I declare that I will render double unto thee;

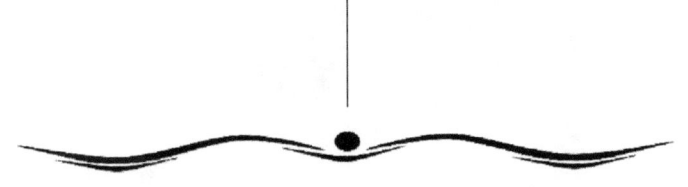

Prayer:

Just as you delivered the prisoners from the pit by the blood, I claim deliverance from recurring sicknesses

Zechariah 9:5-6   **And I Will Strengthen**

5 And they shall be as mighty men, which tread down their enemies in the mire of the streets in the battle: and they shall fight, because the Lord is with them, and the riders on horses shall be confounded.

6 And I will strengthen the house of Judah, and I will save the house of Joseph, and I will bring them again to place them; for I have mercy upon them: and they shall be as though I had not cast them off: for I am the Lord their God, and will hear them.

Prayer:

As the mighty men, which tread down their enemies, I take authority over every disease brought by Satan

# HEALINGS FROM THE BOOK OF
MALACHI

Healing In His Wings — **Malachi 4:1-2**

1 For, behold, the day cometh, that shall burn as an oven; and all the proud, yea, and all that do wickedly, shall be stubble: and the day that cometh shall burn them up, saith the Lord of hosts, that it shall leave them neither root nor branch.

2 But unto you that fear my name shall the Sun of righteousness arise with healing in his wings; and ye shall go forth, and grow up as calves of the stall.

Prayer:

O God, forgive my sins and arise with healing in your wings; that I may go forth, and grow as calves of the stall

THE
NEW TESTAMENT

HEALINGS FROM THE BOOK OF
MATTHEW

Jesus Heals in Syria   **Matthew 4:23-24**

23 And Jesus went about all Galilee, teaching in their synagogues, and preaching the gospel of the kingdom, and healing all manner of sickness and all manner of disease among the people.

24 And his fame went throughout all Syria: and they brought unto him all sick people that were taken with divers diseases and torments, and those which were possessed with devils, and those which were lunatick, and those that had the palsy; and he healed them.

Prayer:

Lord Jesus, you healed all sick people that were taken with divers disease; in like manner I receive my healing

Matthew 8:1-4 *His Leprosy Was Cleansed*

1 When he was come down from the mountain, great multitudes followed him.

2 And, behold, there came a leper and worshipped him, saying, Lord, if thou wilt, thou canst make me clean.

3 And Jesus put forth his hand, and touched him, saying, I will; be thou clean. And immediately his leprosy was cleansed.

4 And Jesus saith unto him, See thou tell no man; but go thy way, shew thyself to the priest, and offer the gift that Moses commanded, for a testimony unto them.

Prayer:

Heavenly Father, it is your will to heal me as sickness is not of God, I therefore claim my complete healing

His Servant Was Healed   Matthew 8:5-12

5 And when Jesus was entered into Capernaum, there came unto him a centurion, beseeching him,

6 And saying, Lord, my servant lieth at home sick of the palsy, grievously tormented.

7 And Jesus saith unto him, I will come and heal him.

8 The centurion answered and said, Lord, I am not worthy that thou shouldest come under my roof: but speak the word only, and my servant shall be healed.

9 For I am a man under authority, having soldiers under me: and I say to this man, Go, and he goeth; and to another, Come, and he cometh; and to my servant, Do this, and he doeth it.

10 When Jesus heard it, he marvelled, and said to them that followed, Verily I say unto you, I have not found so great faith, no, not in Israel.

11 And I say unto you, That many shall come from the east and west, and shall sit down with Abraham, and Isaac, and Jacob, in the kingdom of heaven.

12 But the children of the kingdom shall be cast out into outer darkness: there shall be weeping and gnashing of teeth.

contd.

Matthew 8:13   *His Servant Was Healed*

13 And Jesus said unto the centurion, Go thy way; and as thou hast believed, so be it done unto thee. And his servant was healed in the selfsame hour.

Prayer:

Lord, according to your word, you have provided healing; like the centurion, I believe and receive healing

Himself Took Our Infirmities   **Matthew 8:14-17**

14 And when Jesus was come into Peter's house, he saw his wife's mother laid, and sick of a fever.

15 And he touched her hand, and the fever left her: and she arose, and ministered unto them.

16 When the even was come, they brought unto him many that were possessed with devils: and he cast out the spirits with his word, and healed all that were sick:

17 That it might be fulfilled which was spoken by Esaias the prophet, saying, Himself took our infirmities, and bare our sicknesses.

Prayer:

Jesus you took our infirmities, and bare our sicknesses; I therefore command spirits of sickness to leave my body

Matthew 8:28-33   *And He Said Unto Them, Go*

28 And when he was come to the other side into the country of the Gergesenes, there met him two possessed with devils, coming out of the tombs, exceeding fierce, so that no man might pass by that way.

29 And, behold, they cried out, saying, What have we to do with thee, Jesus, thou Son of God? art thou come hither to torment us before the time?

30 And there was a good way off from them an herd of many swine feeding.

31 So the devils besought him, saying, If thou cast us out, suffer us to go away into the herd of swine.

32 And he said unto them, Go. And when they were come out, they went into the herd of swine: and, behold, the whole herd of swine ran violently down a steep place into the sea, and perished in the waters.

33 And they that kept them fled, and went their ways into the city, and told every thing, and what was befallen to the possessed of the devils.

Prayer:

Father, Jesus cast out devils from the two, I therefore take deliverance from demonic influences in my life

Take Up Thy Bed, And Go — **Matthew 9:1-7**

1 And he entered into a ship, and passed over, and came into his own city.

2 And, behold, they brought to him a man sick of the palsy, lying on a bed: and Jesus seeing their faith said unto the sick of the palsy; Son, be of good cheer; thy sins be forgiven thee.

3 And, behold, certain of the scribes said within themselves, This man blasphemeth.

4 And Jesus knowing their thoughts said, Wherefore think ye evil in your hearts?

5 For whether is easier, to say, Thy sins be forgiven thee; or to say, Arise, and walk?

6 But that ye may know that the Son of man hath power on earth to forgive sins, (then saith he to the sick of the palsy,) Arise, take up thy bed, and go unto thine house.

7 And he arose, and departed to his house.

Prayer:

Dear Lord, I forgive those who offended me, I repent of my sins and ask for your forgiveness and healing

Matthew 9:18-23 — *And The Maid Arose*

18 While he spake these things unto them, behold, there came a certain ruler, and worshipped him, saying, My daughter is even now dead: but come and lay thy hand upon her, and she shall live.

19 And Jesus arose, and followed him, and so did his disciples.

20 And, behold, a woman, which was diseased with an issue of blood twelve years, came behind him, and touched the hem of his garment:

21 For she said within herself, If I may but touch his garment, I shall be whole.

22 But Jesus turned him about, and when he saw her, he said, Daughter, be of good comfort; thy faith hath made thee whole. And the woman was made whole from that hour.

23 And when Jesus came into the ruler's house, and saw the minstrels and the people making a noise,

contd.

And The Maid Arose — Matthew 9:24-25

24 He said unto them, Give place: for the maid is not dead, but sleepeth. And they laughed him to scorn.

25 But when the people were put forth, he went in, and took her by the hand, and the maid arose.

Prayer:

O God who raises the dead, I receive strength and boldness to pray for and raise the dead

Matthew 9:27-33 — *The Dumb Spake*

27 And when Jesus departed thence, two blind men followed him, crying, and saying, Thou son of David, have mercy on us.

28 And when he was come into the house, the blind men came to him: and Jesus saith unto them, Believe ye that I am able to do this? They said unto him, Yea, Lord.

29 Then touched he their eyes, saying, According to your faith be it unto you.

30 And their eyes were opened; and Jesus straitly charged them, saying, See that no man know it.

31 But they, when they were departed, spread abroad his fame in all that country.

32 As they went out, behold, they brought to him a dumb man possessed with a devil.

33 And when the devil was cast out, the dumb spake: and the multitudes marvelled, saying, It was never so seen in Israel.

Prayer:

Almighty God I thank you for authority; in Jesus name I receive healing and rebuke every devil of sickness in me

Heal The Sick, Cleanse The Lepers   Matthew 10:5-8

5 These twelve Jesus sent forth, and commanded them, saying, Go not into the way of the Gentiles, and into any city of the Samaritans enter ye not:

6 But go rather to the lost sheep of the house of Israel.

7 And as ye go, preach, saying, The kingdom of heaven is at hand.

8 Heal the sick, cleanse the lepers, raise the dead, cast out devils: freely ye have received, freely give.

Prayer:

Lord Jesus, I receive grace to preach the kingdom of heaven, heal the sick, raise the dead, and cast out devils

Matthew 11:4-6   *The Blind Receive Their Sight*

4 Jesus answered and said unto them, Go and shew John again those things which ye do hear and see:

5 The blind receive their sight, and the lame walk, the lepers are cleansed, and the deaf hear, the dead are raised up, and the poor have the gospel preached to them.

6 And blessed is he, whosoever shall not be offended in me.

Prayer:

Lord I pray that the blind see, the lame walk, the deaf hear, the dead be raised, and the poor hear the gospel

Man With The Withered Hand — Matthew 12:9-13

9 And when he was departed thence, he went into their synagogue:

10 And, behold, there was a man which had his hand withered. And they asked him, saying, Is it lawful to heal on the sabbath days? that they might accuse him.

11 And he said unto them, What man shall there be among you, that shall have one sheep, and if it fall into a pit on the sabbath day, will he not lay hold on it, and lift it out?

12 How much then is a man better than a sheep? Wherefore it is lawful to do well on the sabbath days.

13 Then saith he to the man, Stretch forth thine hand. And he stretched it forth; and it was restored whole, like as the other.

Prayer:

Father I receive grace to obey your word; I stretch forth my arms as I manifest the healing you have provided

Matthew 12:20-22 — *And He Healed Him*

20 A bruised reed shall he not break, and smoking flax shall he not quench, till he send forth judgment unto victory.

21 And in his name shall the Gentiles trust.

22 Then was brought unto him one possessed with a devil, blind, and dumb: and he healed him, insomuch that the blind and dumb both spake and saw.

Prayer:

Just like Jesus, I pray for patience with people around me and for compassion to heal the sick and rebuke devils

He Healed Their Sick — **Matthew 14:13-14**

13 When Jesus heard of it, he departed thence by ship into a desert place apart: and when the people had heard thereof, they followed him on foot out of the cities.

14 And Jesus went forth, and saw a great multitude, and was moved with compassion toward them, and he healed their sick.

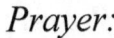

Prayer:

*Jesus, in your love and compassion
I believe you want me well; I therefore claim
my healing and resist the devil*

Matthew 14:34-36 *Made Perfectly Whole*

34 And when they were gone over, they came into the land of Gennesaret.

35 And when the men of that place had knowledge of him, they sent out into all that country round about, and brought unto him all that were diseased;

36 And besought him that they might only touch the hem of his garment: and as many as touched were made perfectly whole.

Prayer:

O faithful God, Jesus healed all the diseased brought to him, I come as one of these and I too receive my healing

Woman, Great Is Thy Faith   Matthew 15:22-28

22 And, behold, a woman of Canaan came out of the same coasts, and cried unto him, saying, Have mercy on me, O Lord, thou son of David; my daughter is grievously vexed with a devil.

23 But he answered her not a word. And his disciples came and besought him, saying, Send her away; for she crieth after us.

24 But he answered and said, I am not sent but unto the lost sheep of the house of Israel.

25 Then came she and worshipped him, saying, Lord, help me.

26 But he answered and said, It is not meet to take the children's bread, and to cast it to dogs.

27 And she said, Truth, Lord: yet the dogs eat of the crumbs which fall from their masters' table.

28 Then Jesus answered and said unto her, O woman, great is thy faith: be it unto thee even as thou wilt. And her daughter was made whole from that very hour.

Prayer:

Merciful Lord, help me humble myself and persist in faith, for you are full of mercy and compassion

Matthew 15:29-31 *Jesus Heals Great Multitudes*

29 And Jesus departed from thence, and came nigh unto the sea of Galilee; and went up into a mountain, and sat down there.

30 And great multitudes came unto him, having with them those that were lame, blind, dumb, maimed, and many others, and cast them down at Jesus' feet; and he healed them:

31 Insomuch that the multitude wondered, when they saw the dumb to speak, the maimed to be whole, the lame to walk, and the blind to see: and they glorified the God of Israel.

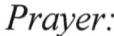

Prayer:

You are the same yesterday and today, you healed the dumb, lame, blind; I likewise receive my healing today

And The Child Was Cured Matthew 17:14-18

14 And when they were come to the multitude, there came to him a certain man, kneeling down to him, and saying,

15 Lord, have mercy on my son: for he is lunatick, and sore vexed: for ofttimes he falleth into the fire, and oft into the water.

16 And I brought him to thy disciples, and they could not cure him.

17 Then Jesus answered and said, O faithless and perverse generation, how long shall I be with you? how long shall I suffer you? bring him hither to me.

18 And Jesus rebuked the devil; and he departed out of him: and the child was cured from that very hour.

Prayer:

According to the word of God regarding my authority, in the name of JESUS I command you devil to leave

Matthew 18:18-20 *It Shall Be Done For Them*

18 Verily I say unto you, Whatsoever ye shall bind on earth shall be bound in heaven: and whatsoever ye shall loose on earth shall be loosed in heaven.

19 Again I say unto you, That if two of you shall agree on earth as touching any thing that they shall ask, it shall be done for them of my Father which is in heaven.

20 For where two or three are gathered together in my name, there am I in the midst of them.

Prayer:

In the name of JESUS I bind the devil and loose God's blessings; in agreement with the word I receive healing

Jesus Heals The Multitudes — Matthew 19:1-2

1 And it came to pass, that when Jesus had finished these sayings, he departed from Galilee, and came into the coasts of Judaea beyond Jordan;

2 And great multitudes followed him; and he healed them there.

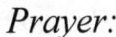

Prayer:

Lord Jesus I thank you for paying the price for me according to your teaching and now I receive my healing

Matthew 20:29-34 — *Blind Men Received Sight*

29 And as they departed from Jericho, a great multitude followed him.

30 And, behold, two blind men sitting by the way side, when they heard that Jesus passed by, cried out, saying, Have mercy on us, O Lord, thou son of David.

31 And the multitude rebuked them, because they should hold their peace: but they cried the more, saying, Have mercy on us, O Lord, thou son of David.

32 And Jesus stood still, and called them, and said, What will ye that I shall do unto you?

33 They say unto him, Lord, that our eyes may be opened.

34 So Jesus had compassion on them, and touched their eyes: and immediately their eyes received sight, and they followed him.

Prayer:

O Lord have mercy on me; in your compassion heal me from this weakness, sickness and disease in Jesus name

Jesus Heals The Blind And Lame Matthew 21:13-15

13 And said unto them, It is written, My house shall be called the house of prayer; but ye have made it a den of thieves.

14 And the blind and the lame came to him in the temple; and he healed them.

15 And when the chief priests and scribes saw the wonderful things that he did, and the children crying in the temple, and saying, Hosanna to the son of David; they were sore displeased,

Prayer:

Jesus Christ the Son of God, I come into your house to ask for and receive healing from all sickness and disease

Matthew 21:19-22 — *The Fig Tree*

19 And when he saw a fig tree in the way, he came to it, and found nothing thereon, but leaves only, and said unto it, Let no fruit grow on thee henceforward for ever.

And presently the fig tree withered away.

20 And when the disciples saw it, they marvelled, saying, How soon is the fig tree withered away!

21 Jesus answered and said unto them, Verily I say unto you, If ye have faith, and doubt not, ye shall not only do this which is done to the fig tree, but also if ye shall say unto this mountain, Be thou removed, and be thou cast into the sea; it shall be done.

22 And all things, whatsoever ye shall ask in prayer, believing, ye shall receive.

Prayer:

I curse the root of every diseased tissue in my body; I command it to die and leave to return no more

Jesus Gives Life In Death — Matthew 27:48-53

48 And straightway one of them ran, and took a spunge, and filled it with vinegar, and put it on a reed, and gave him to drink.

49 The rest said, Let be, let us see whether Elias will come to save him.

50 Jesus, when he had cried again with a loud voice, yielded up the ghost.

51 And, behold, the veil of the temple was rent in twain from the top to the bottom; and the earth did quake, and the rocks rent;

52 And the graves were opened; and many bodies of the saints which slept arose,

53 And came out of the graves after his resurrection, and went into the holy city, and appeared unto many.

Prayer:

Thank you Lord for the victory of the cross; now the sick are healed and the dead shall rise; I receive my healing

HEALINGS FROM THE BOOK OF
MARK

The Unclean Spirit   **Mark 1:23-26**

23 And there was in their synagogue a man with an unclean spirit; and he cried out,

24 Saying, Let us alone; what have we to do with thee, thou Jesus of Nazareth? art thou come to destroy us? I know thee who thou art, the Holy One of God.

25 And Jesus rebuked him, saying, Hold thy peace, and come out of him.

26 And when the unclean spirit had torn him, and cried with a loud voice, he came out of him.

Prayer:

I rebuke you unclean spirit and command you to come out of me and my loved ones

Mark 1:29-34 — *Jesus Heals Diseases*

29 And forthwith, when they were come out of the synagogue, they entered into the house of Simon and Andrew, with James and John.

30 But Simon's wife's mother lay sick of a fever, and anon they tell him of her.

31 And he came and took her by the hand, and lifted her up; and immediately the fever left her, and she ministered unto them.

32 And at even, when the sun did set, they brought unto him all that were diseased, and them that were possessed with devils.

33 And all the city was gathered together at the door.

34 And he healed many that were sick of divers diseases, and cast out many devils; and suffered not the devils to speak, because they knew him.

Prayer:

I command devils to be cast out of those possessed with devils and I speak healing to those sick of divers diseases

The Leprosy Departed — Mark 1:39-42

39 And he preached in their synagogues throughout all Galilee, and cast out devils.

40 And there came a leper to him, beseeching him, and kneeling down to him, and saying unto him, If thou wilt, thou canst make me clean.

41 And Jesus, moved with compassion, put forth his hand, and touched him, and saith unto him, I will; be thou clean.

42 And as soon as he had spoken, immediately the leprosy departed from him, and he was cleansed.

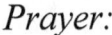

Prayer:

*Lord thank you for your compassion,
I know it is your will for me to be healed;
I therefore receive my healing*

Mark 2:2-9 — *Jesus Heals The Sick Of Palsy*

2 And straightway many were gathered together, insomuch that there was no room to receive them, no, not so much as about the door: and he preached the word unto them.

6 But there was certain of the scribes sitting there, and reasoning in their hearts,

3 And they come unto him, bringing one sick of the palsy, which was borne of four.

4 And when they could not come nigh unto him for the press, they uncovered the roof where he was: and when they had broken it up, they let down the bed wherein the sick of the palsy lay.

5 When Jesus saw their faith, he said unto the sick of the palsy, Son, thy sins be forgiven thee.

7 Why doth this man thus speak blasphemies? who can forgive sins but God only?

8 And immediately when Jesus perceived in his spirit that they so reasoned within themselves, he said unto them, Why reason ye these things in your hearts?

9 Whether is it easier to say to the sick of the palsy, Thy sins be forgiven thee; or to say, Arise, and take up thy bed, and walk?

contd.

The Sick Of The Palsy — **Mark 2:10-12**

10 But that ye may know that the Son of man hath power on earth to forgive sins, (he saith to the sick of the palsy,)

11 I say unto thee, Arise, and take up thy bed, and go thy way into thine house.

12 And immediately he arose, took up the bed, and went forth before them all; insomuch that they were all amazed, and glorified God, saying, We never saw it on this fashion.

Prayer:

Lord, I repent of my sins and I thank you for forgiving me; I receive healing in my body and go my way healed

Mark 3:1-5 — *Jesus Heals The Withered Hand*

1 And he entered again into the synagogue; and there was a man there which had a withered hand.

2 And they watched him, whether he would heal him on the sabbath day; that they might accuse him.

3 And he saith unto the man which had the withered hand, Stand forth.

4 And he saith unto them, Is it lawful to do good on the sabbath days, or to do evil? to save life, or to kill? But they held their peace.

5 And when he had looked round about on them with anger, being grieved for the hardness of their hearts, he saith unto the man, Stretch forth thine hand. And he stretched it out: and his hand was restored whole as the other.

Prayer:

Thank you Lord for you are willing to heal me despite oppositions; I take my healing according to your word

Jesus Heals Many   **Mark 3:10-12**

10 For he had healed many; insomuch that they pressed upon him for to touch him, as many as had plagues.

11 And unclean spirits, when they saw him, fell down before him, and cried, saying, Thou art the Son of God.

12 And he straitly charged them that they should not make him known.

Prayer:

Dear Lord, I reach out to you for healing from the outbreak of diseases in my community; I resist the devil

Mark 5:2-10 — *Jesus Cast Out Unclean Spirit*

2 And when he was come out of the ship, immediately there met him out of the tombs a man with an unclean spirit,

3 Who had his dwelling among the tombs; and no man could bind him, no, not with chains:

4 Because that he had been often bound with fetters and chains, and the chains had been plucked asunder by him, and the fetters broken in pieces: neither could any man tame him.

5 And always, night and day, he was in the mountains, and in the tombs, crying, and cutting himself with stones.

6 But when he saw Jesus afar off, he ran and worshipped him,

7 And cried with a loud voice, and said, What have I to do with thee, Jesus, thou Son of the most high God? I adjure thee by God, that thou torment me not.

8 For he said unto him, Come out of the man, thou unclean spirit.

9 And he asked him, What is thy name? And he answered, saying, My name is Legion: for we are many.

10 And he besought him much that he would not send them away out of the country.

contd.

Jesus Cast Out Unclean Spirit — Mark 5:11-15

11 Now there was there nigh unto the mountains a great herd of swine feeding.

12 And all the devils besought him, saying, Send us into the swine, that we may enter into them.

13 And forthwith Jesus gave them leave. And the unclean spirits went out, and entered into the swine: and the herd ran violently down a steep place into the sea, (they were about two thousand;) and were choked in the sea.

14 And they that fed the swine fled, and told it in the city, and in the country. And they went out to see what it was that was done.

15 And they come to Jesus, and see him that was possessed with the devil, and had the legion, sitting, and clothed, and in his right mind: and they were afraid.

Prayer:

In the name of Jesus, I command the unclean spirit which has been tormenting me to get out of me never to return

Mark 5:22-30   *Issue of Blood And Jarius's Daughter*

22 And, behold, there cometh one of the rulers of the synagogue, Jairus by name; and when he saw him, he fell at his feet,

23 And besought him greatly, saying, My little daughter lieth at the point of death: I pray thee, come and lay thy hands on her, that she may be healed; and she shall live.

24 And Jesus went with him; and much people followed him, and thronged him.

25 And a certain woman, which had an issue of blood twelve years,

26 And had suffered many things of many physicians, and had spent all that she had, and was nothing bettered, but rather grew worse,

27 When she had heard of Jesus, came in the press behind, and touched his garment.

28 For she said, If I may touch but his clothes, I shall be whole.

29 And straightway the fountain of her blood was dried up; and she felt in her body that she was healed of that plague.

30 And Jesus, immediately knowing in himself that virtue had gone out of him, turned him about in the press, and said, Who touched my clothes?

contd.

Issue of Blood And Jarius's Daughter Mark 5:31-39

31 And his disciples said unto him, Thou seest the multitude thronging thee, and sayest thou, Who touched me?

32 And he looked round about to see her that had done this thing.

33 But the woman fearing and trembling, knowing what was done in her, came and fell down before him, and told him all the truth.

34 And he said unto her, Daughter, thy faith hath made thee whole; go in peace, and be whole of thy plague.

35 While he yet spake, there came from the ruler of the synagogue's house certain which said, Thy daughter is dead: why troublest thou the Master any further?

36 As soon as Jesus heard the word that was spoken, he saith unto the ruler of the synagogue, Be not afraid, only believe.

37 And he suffered no man to follow him, save Peter, and James, and John the brother of James.

38 And he cometh to the house of the ruler of the synagogue, and seeth the tumult, and them that wept and wailed greatly.

39 And when he was come in, he saith unto them, Why make ye this ado, and weep? the damsel is not dead, but sleepeth.

contd.

Mark 5:40-42 *Issue of Blood And Jarius's Daughter*

40 And they laughed him to scorn. But when he had put them all out, he taketh the father and the mother of the damsel, and them that were with him, and entereth in where the damsel was lying.

41 And he took the damsel by the hand, and said unto her, Talitha cumi; which is, being interpreted, Damsel, I say unto thee, arise.

42 And straightway the damsel arose, and walked; for she was of the age of twelve years. And they were astonished with a great astonishment.

Prayer:

O God who heals the sick and raises the dead, like the woman, I take my healing and I speak life to the dead

Danger Of Unbelief

Mark 6:4-6

4 But Jesus, said unto them, A prophet is not without honour, but in his own country, and among his own kin, and in his own house.

5 And he could there do no mighty work, save that he laid his hands upon a few sick folk, and healed them.

6 And he marvelled because of their unbelief. And he went round about the villages, teaching.

Prayer:

O Lord I believe, help my unbelief so that I do not miss receiving my healing; teach me through your word

Mark 6:53-56 *Jesus Heals The Sick*

53 And when they had passed over, they came into the land of Gennesaret, and drew to the shore.

54 And when they were come out of the ship, straightway they knew him,

55 And ran through that whole region round about, and began to carry about in beds those that were sick, where they heard he was.

56 And whithersoever he entered, into villages, or cities, or country, they laid the sick in the streets, and besought him that they might touch if it were but the border of his garment: and as many as touched him were made whole.

Prayer:

Jesus, as you were willing to heal the sick who touched you in the streets of Gennesaret, I touch and take healing

The Syrophenician Woman — Mark 7:25-30

25 For a certain woman, whose young daughter had an unclean spirit, heard of him, and came and fell at his feet:

26 The woman was a Greek, a Syrophenician by nation; and she besought him that he would cast forth the devil out of her daughter.

27 But Jesus said unto her, Let the children first be filled: for it is not meet to take the children's bread, and to cast it unto the dogs.

28 And she answered and said unto him, Yes, Lord: yet the dogs under the table eat of the children's crumbs.

29 And he said unto her, For this saying go thy way; the devil is gone out of thy daughter.

30 And when she was come to her house, she found the devil gone out, and her daughter laid upon the bed.

Prayer:

Father forgive me for lack of humility and persistence in prayer; heal my loved one I pray; thank you Lord

Mark 7:32-35   *Jesus Heals The Deaf And Dumb*

32 And they bring unto him one that was deaf, and had an impediment in his speech; and they beseech him to put his hand upon him.

33 And he took him aside from the multitude, and put his fingers into his ears, and he spit, and touched his tongue;

34 And looking up to heaven, he sighed, and saith unto him, Ephphatha, that is, Be opened.

35 And straightway his ears were opened, and the string of his tongue was loosed, and he spake plain.

Prayer:

Almighty God, you heal through many ways, I receive your touch on my diseased body part and speak healing

Jesus Heals The Blind Man — **Mark 8:22-25**

22 And he cometh to Bethsaida; and they bring a blind man unto him, and besought him to touch him.

23 And he took the blind man by the hand, and led him out of the town; and when he had spit on his eyes, and put his hands upon him, he asked him if he saw ought.

24 And he looked up, and said, I see men as trees, walking.

25 After that he put his hands again upon his eyes, and made him look up: and he was restored, and saw every man clearly.

Prayer:

Thank you Jesus for by your stripes I am healed; I resist the devil holding fast to my confession till manifestation

Mark 9:17-24 — *Jesus Cast Out Dumb Spirit*

17 And one of the multitude answered and said, Master, I have brought unto thee my son, which hath a dumb spirit;

18 And wheresoever he taketh him, he teareth him: and he foameth, and gnasheth with his teeth, and pineth away: and I spake to thy disciples that they should cast him out; and they could not.

19 He answereth him, and saith, O faithless generation, how long shall I be with you? how long shall I suffer you? bring him unto me.

20 And they brought him unto him: and when he saw him, straightway the spirit tare him; and he fell on the ground, and wallowed foaming.

21 And he asked his father, How long is it ago since this came unto him? And he said, Of a child.

22 And ofttimes it hath cast him into the fire, and into the waters, to destroy him: but if thou canst do any thing, have compassion on us, and help us.

23 Jesus said unto him, If thou canst believe, all things are possible to him that believeth.

24 And straightway the father of the child cried out, and said with tears, Lord, I believe; help thou mine unbelief

contd.

Jesus Cast Out Dumb Spirit — Mark 9:25-29

25 When Jesus saw that the people came running together, he rebuked the foul spirit, saying unto him, Thou dumb and deaf spirit, I charge thee, come out of him, and enter no more into him.

26 And the spirit cried, and rent him sore, and came out of him: and he was as one dead; insomuch that many said, He is dead.

27 But Jesus took him by the hand, and lifted him up; and he arose.

28 And when he was come into the house, his disciples asked him privately, Why could not we cast him out?

29 And he said unto them, This kind can come forth by nothing, but by prayer and fasting.

Prayer:

*Lord, I believe; help thou mine unbelief;
I receive grace to pray and fast and in faith,
cast out every unclean spirit*

Mark 10:46-51 *Jesus Heals Blind Bartimaeus*

46 And they came to Jericho: and as he went out of Jericho with his disciples and a great number of people, blind Bartimaeus, the son of Timaeus, sat by the highway side begging.

47 And when he heard that it was Jesus of Nazareth, he began to cry out, and say, Jesus, thou son of David, have mercy on me.

48 And many charged him that he should hold his peace: but he cried the more a great deal, Thou son of David, have mercy on me.

49 And Jesus stood still, and commanded him to be called. And they call the blind man, saying unto him, Be of good comfort, rise; he calleth thee.

50 And he, casting away his garment, rose, and came to Jesus.

51 And Jesus answered and said unto him, What wilt thou that I should do unto thee? The blind man said unto him, Lord, that I might receive my sight.

contd.

Jesus Heals Blind Bartimaeus — Mark 10:52

52 And Jesus said unto him, Go thy way; thy faith hath made thee whole. And immediately he received his sight, and followed Jesus in the way.

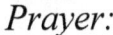

Prayer:

Jesus, son of the living God, have mercy on me; I receive healing in the afflicted part of my body and I thank you

Mark 11:12-14; 20-23 — *The Fig Tree*

12 And on the morrow, when they were come from Bethany, he was hungry:

13 And seeing a fig tree afar off having leaves, he came, if haply he might find any thing thereon: and when he came to it, he found nothing but leaves; for the time of figs was not yet.

14 And Jesus answered and said unto it, No man eat fruit of thee hereafter for ever. And his disciples heard it.

20 And in the morning, as they passed by, they saw the fig tree dried up from the roots.

21 And Peter calling to remembrance saith unto him, Master, behold, the fig tree which thou cursedst is withered away.

22 And Jesus answering saith unto them, Have faith in God.

23 For verily I say unto you, That whosoever shall say unto this mountain, Be thou removed, and be thou cast into the sea; and shall not doubt in his heart, but shall believe that those things which he saith shall come to pass; he shall have whatsoever he saith.

contd.

The Fig Tree — Mark 11:24-26

24 Therefore I say unto you, What things soever ye desire, when ye pray, believe that ye receive them, and ye shall have them.

25 And when ye stand praying, forgive, if ye have ought against any: that your Father also which is in heaven may forgive you your trespasses.

26 But if ye do not forgive, neither will your Father which is in heaven forgive your trespasses.

Prayer:

Lord, I desire healing in my body, I believe I receive healing and I thank you even if manifestation is pending

HEALINGS FROM THE BOOK OF
LUKE

Spirit Of An Unclean Devil — Luke 4:33-36

33 And in the synagogue there was a man, which had a spirit of an unclean devil, and cried out with a loud voice,

34 Saying, Let us alone; what have we to do with thee, thou Jesus of Nazareth? art thou come to destroy us? I know thee who thou art; the Holy One of God.

35 And Jesus rebuked him, saying, Hold thy peace, and come out of him. And when the devil had thrown him in the midst, he came out of him, and hurt him not.

36 And they were all amazed, and spake among themselves, saying, What a word is this! for with authority and power he commandeth the unclean spirits, and they come out.

Prayer:

You unclean devil, I command you in the name of Jesus, come out of this body; thank you Lord

Luke 4:38-39   *Simon's wife's mother*

38 And he arose out of the synagogue, and entered into Simon's house. And Simon's wife's mother was taken with a great fever; and they besought him for her.

39 And he stood over her, and rebuked the fever; and it left her: and immediately she arose and ministered unto them.

Prayer:

You fever and sickness, I rebuke you in the name of Jesus, you will leave and never return

Devils Also Came Out Of Many — Luke 4:40-42

40 Now when the sun was setting, all they that had any sick with divers diseases brought them unto him; and he laid his hands on every one of them, and healed them.

41 And devils also came out of many, crying out, and saying, Thou art Christ the Son of God. And he rebuking them suffered them not to speak: for they knew that he was Christ.

42 And when it was day, he departed and went into a desert place: and the people sought him, and came unto him, and stayed him, that he should not depart from them.

Prayer:

Dear God, as the elders in the church lay hands on me, I receive my healing and receive deliverance from devils

Luke 5:12-15 — *A Man Full Of Leprosy*

12 And it came to pass, when he was in a certain city, behold a man full of leprosy: who seeing Jesus fell on his face, and besought him, saying, Lord, if thou wilt, thou canst make me clean.

13 And he put forth his hand, and touched him, saying, I will: be thou clean. And immediately the leprosy departed from him.

14 And he charged him to tell no man: but go, and shew thyself to the priest, and offer for thy cleansing, according as Moses commanded, for a testimony unto them.

15 But so much the more went there a fame abroad of him: and great multitudes came together to hear, and to be healed by him of their infirmities.

Prayer:

I thank you Lord for you are always willing to heal; I receive your healing touch in my body by faith

Jesus Heals Man With Palsy — Luke 5:17-23

17 And it came to pass on a certain day, as he was teaching, that there were Pharisees and doctors of the law sitting by, which were come out of every town of Galilee, and Judaea, and Jerusalem: and the power of the Lord was present to heal them.

18 And, behold, men brought in a bed a man which was taken with a palsy: and they sought means to bring him in, and to lay him before him.

19 And when they could not find by what way they might bring him in because of the multitude, they went upon the housetop, and let him down through the tiling with his couch into the midst before Jesus.

20 And when he saw their faith, he said unto him, Man, thy sins are forgiven thee.

21 And the scribes and the Pharisees began to reason, saying, Who is this which speaketh blasphemies? Who can forgive sins, but God alone?

22 But when Jesus perceived their thoughts, he answering said unto them, What reason ye in your hearts?

23 Whether is easier, to say, Thy sins be forgiven thee; or to say, Rise up and walk?

contd.

Luke 5:24-25 — *Jesus Heals Man With Palsy*

24 But that ye may know that the Son of man hath power upon earth to forgive sins, (he said unto the sick of the palsy,) I say unto thee, Arise, and take up thy couch, and go into thine house.

25 And immediately he rose up before them, and took up that whereon he lay, and departed to his own house, glorifying God.

Prayer:

Father forgive my wrongs I pray;
Lord Jesus, as I take this step of faith,
may your power rest on me to heal

Man With Withered Hand — Luke 6:6-10

6 And it came to pass also on another sabbath, that he entered into the synagogue and taught: and there was a man whose right hand was withered.

7 And the scribes and Pharisees watched him, whether he would heal on the sabbath day; that they might find an accusation against him.

8 But he knew their thoughts, and said to the man which had the withered hand, Rise up, and stand forth in the midst. And he arose and stood forth.

9 Then said Jesus unto them, I will ask you one thing; Is it lawful on the sabbath days to do good, or to do evil? to save life, or to destroy it?

10 And looking round about upon them all, he said unto the man, Stretch forth thy hand. And he did so: and his hand was restored whole as the other.

Prayer:

Jesus thank you for your willingness to save and heal at all times; I stretch forth my hand and receive healing

Luke 6:17-19 — *Jesus Heals Them All*

17 And he came down with them, and stood in the plain, and the company of his disciples, and a great multitude of people out of all Judaea and Jerusalem, and from the sea coast of Tyre and Sidon, which came to hear him, and to be healed of their diseases;

18 And they that were vexed with unclean spirits: and they were healed.

19 And the whole multitude sought to touch him: for there went virtue out of him, and healed them all.

Prayer:

*Lord I need to hear and be healed;
help me understand as I read your word,
believe and touch you and be healed*

The Centurion's Servant — Luke 7:2-8

2 And a certain centurion's servant, who was dear unto him, was sick, and ready to die.

3 And when he heard of Jesus, he sent unto him the elders of the Jews, beseeching him that he would come and heal his servant.

4 And when they came to Jesus, they besought him instantly, saying, That he was worthy for whom he should do this:

5 For he loveth our nation, and he hath built us a synagogue.

6 Then Jesus went with them. And when he was now not far from the house, the centurion sent friends to him, saying unto him, Lord, trouble not thyself: for I am not worthy that thou shouldest enter under my roof:

7 Wherefore neither thought I myself worthy to come unto thee: but say in a word, and my servant shall be healed.

8 For I also am a man set under authority, having under me soldiers, and I say unto one, Go, and he goeth; and to another, Come, and he cometh; and to my servant, Do this, and he doeth it.

contd.

Luke 7:9-10 — *The Centurion's Servant*

9 When Jesus heard these things, he marvelled at him, and turned him about, and said unto the people that followed him, I say unto you, I have not found so great faith, no, not in Israel.

10 And they that were sent, returning to the house, found the servant whole that had been sick.

Prayer:

Father thank you for you sent your word and healed me; may it be unto me according to what and how I believe

Jesus Raises The Dead   **Luke 7:11-16**

11 And it came to pass the day after, that he went into a city called Nain; and many of his disciples went with him, and much people.

12 Now when he came nigh to the gate of the city, behold, there was a dead man carried out, the only son of his mother, and she was a widow: and much people of the city was with her.

13 And when the Lord saw her, he had compassion on her, and said unto her, Weep not.

14 And he came and touched the bier: and they that bare him stood still.

And he said, Young man, I say unto thee, Arise.

15 And he that was dead sat up, and began to speak. And he delivered him to his mother.

16 And there came a fear on all: and they glorified God, saying, That a great prophet is risen up among us; and, That God hath visited his people.

Prayer:

O God of heavens who heals the sick and raises the dead, hear my prayer this day; now I speak to the dead, arise!

Luke 8:26-32 *Jesus Heals The Devil-Possessed*

26 And they arrived at the country of the Gadarenes, which is over against Galilee.

27 And when he went forth to land, there met him out of the city a certain man, which had devils long time, and ware no clothes, neither abode in any house, but in the tombs.

28 When he saw Jesus, he cried out, and fell down before him, and with a loud voice said, What have I to do with thee, Jesus, thou Son of God most high? I beseech thee, torment me not.

29 (For he had commanded the unclean spirit to come out of the man. For oftentimes it had caught him: and he was kept bound with chains and in fetters; and he brake the bands, and was driven of the devil into the wilderness.)

30 And Jesus asked him, saying, What is thy name? And he said, Legion: because many devils were entered into him.

31 And they besought him that he would not command them to go out into the deep.

32 And there was there an herd of many swine feeding on the mountain: and they besought him that he would suffer them to enter into them. And he suffered them.

contd.

Jesus Heals The Devil-Possessed — Luke 8:33-36

33 Then went the devils out of the man, and entered into the swine: and the herd ran violently down a steep place into the lake, and were choked.

34 When they that fed them saw what was done, they fled, and went and told it in the city and in the country.

35 Then they went out to see what was done; and came to Jesus, and found the man, out of whom the devils were departed, sitting at the feet of Jesus, clothed, and in his right mind: and they were afraid.

36 They also which saw it told them by what means he that was possessed of the devils was healed.

Prayer:

You devils, in the name of Jesus I command you to go out of this person and you will never return

Luke 8:40-46 *Jesus Heals And Raises the Dead*

40 And it came to pass, that, when Jesus was returned, the people gladly received him: for they were all waiting for him.

41 And, behold, there came a man named Jairus, and he was a ruler of the synagogue: and he fell down at Jesus' feet, and besought him that he would come into his house:

42 For he had one only daughter, about twelve years of age, and she lay a dying. But as he went the people thronged him.

43 And a woman having an issue of blood twelve years, which had spent all her living upon physicians, neither could be healed of any,

44 Came behind him, and touched the border of his garment: and immediately her issue of blood stanched.

45 And Jesus said, Who touched me? When all denied, Peter and they that were with him said, Master, the multitude throng thee and press thee, and sayest thou, Who touched me?

46 And Jesus said, Somebody hath touched me: for I perceive that virtue is gone out of me.

contd.

Jesus Heals And Raises the Dead   Luke 8:47-54

47 And when the woman saw that she was not hid, she came trembling, and falling down before him, she declared unto him before all the people for what cause she had touched him, and how she was healed immediately.

48 And he said unto her, Daughter, be of good comfort: thy faith hath made thee whole; go in peace.

49 While he yet spake, there cometh one from the ruler of the synagogue's house, saying to him, Thy daughter is dead; trouble not the Master.

50 But when Jesus heard it, he answered him, saying, Fear not: believe only, and she shall be made whole.

51 And when he came into the house, he suffered no man to go in, save Peter, and James, and John, and the father and the mother of the maiden.

52 And all wept, and bewailed her: but he said, Weep not; she is not dead, but sleepeth.

53 And they laughed him to scorn, knowing that she was dead.

54 And he put them all out, and took her by the hand, and called, saying, Maid, arise.

contd.

Luke 8:55-56   *Jesus Heals And Raises the Dead*

55 And her spirit came again, and she arose straightway: and he commanded to give her meat.

56 And her parents were astonished: but he charged them that they should tell no man what was done.

Prayer:

Lord Jesus, you are able to heal the sick and raise the dead; I take my healing and speak life to anything dead

Jesus Healed Everywhere — Luke 9:1-6

1 Then he called his twelve disciples together, and gave them power and authority over all devils, and to cure diseases.

2 And he sent them to preach the kingdom of God, and to heal the sick.

3 And he said unto them, Take nothing for your journey, neither staves, nor scrip, neither bread, neither money; neither have two coats apiece.

4 And whatsoever house ye enter into, there abide, and thence depart.

5 And whosoever will not receive you, when ye go out of that city, shake off the very dust from your feet for a testimony against them.

6 And they departed, and went through the towns, preaching the gospel, and healing every where.

Prayer:

Thank you Lord for power and authority over all devils, and to cure disease as I exercise it in myself and others

Luke 9:9-11 — *Jesus Healed Those In Need*

9 And Herod said, John have I beheaded: but who is this, of whom I hear such things? And he desired to see him.

10 And the apostles, when they were returned, told him all that they had done. And he took them, and went aside privately into a desert place belonging to the city called Bethsaida.

11 And the people, when they knew it, followed him: and he received them, and spake unto them of the kingdom of God, and healed them that had need of healing.

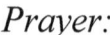

Prayer:

Merciful Lord, healing is a need and you supply our needs; I receive my healing as supplied in your word

Jesus Rebuked The Unclean Spirit   Luke 9:37-42

37 And it came to pass, that on the next day, when they were come down from the hill, much people met him.

38 And, behold, a man of the company cried out, saying, Master, I beseech thee, look upon my son: for he is mine only child.

39 And, lo, a spirit taketh him, and he suddenly crieth out; and it teareth him that he foameth again, and bruising him hardly departeth from him.

40 And I besought thy disciples to cast him out; and they could not.

41 And Jesus answering said, O faithless and perverse generation, how long shall I be with you, and suffer you? Bring thy son hither.

42 And as he was yet a coming, the devil threw him down, and tare him. And Jesus rebuked the unclean spirit, and healed the child, and delivered him again to his father.

Prayer:

I rebuke you unclean spirit and I take my healing and my deliverance from the power of darkness

Luke 10:1-7 — *Heal The Sick That Are Therein*

1 After these things the Lord appointed other seventy also, and sent them two and two before his face into every city and place, whither he himself would come.

2 Therefore said he unto them, The harvest truly is great, but the labourers are few: pray ye therefore the Lord of the harvest, that he would send forth labourers into his harvest.

3 Go your ways: behold, I send you forth as lambs among wolves.

4 Carry neither purse, nor scrip, nor shoes: and salute no man by the way.

5 And into whatsoever house ye enter, first say, Peace be to this house.

6 And if the son of peace be there, your peace shall rest upon it: if not, it shall turn to you again.

7 And in the same house remain, eating and drinking such things as they give: for the labourer is worthy of his hire. Go not from house to house.

contd.

Heal The Sick That Are Therein   **Luke 10:8-9**

8 And into whatsoever city ye enter, and they receive you, eat such things as are set before you:

9 And heal the sick that are therein, and say unto them, The kingdom of God is come nigh unto you.

Prayer:

I go O Lord to preach as you have sent me; may your power be present to heal any in need of healing

Luke 10:17-20   *The Devils Are Subject Unto Us*

17 And the seventy returned again with joy, saying, Lord, even the devils are subject unto us through thy name.

18 And he said unto them, I beheld Satan as lightning fall from heaven.

19 Behold, I give unto you power to tread on serpents and scorpions, and over all the power of the enemy: and nothing shall by any means hurt you.

20 Notwithstanding in this rejoice not, that the spirits are subject unto you; but rather rejoice, because your names are written in heaven.

Prayer:

I tread on serpents scorpions, and over all the power of the enemy in my health and that of my loved ones

Jesus Cast Out A Devil — Luke 11:13-14

13 If ye then, being evil, know how to give good gifts unto your children: how much more shall your heavenly Father give the Holy Spirit to them that ask him?

14 And he was casting out a devil, and it was dumb. And it came to pass, when the devil was gone out, the dumb spake; and the people wondered.

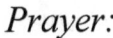

Prayer:

You spirit of sickness, disease and infirmity, I command you in the name of Jesus to come out

Luke 13:10-13 *Woman With A Spirit Of Infirmity*

10 And he was teaching in one of the synagogues on the sabbath.

11 And, behold, there was a woman which had a spirit of infirmity eighteen years, and was bowed together, and could in no wise lift up herself.

12 And when Jesus saw her, he called her to him, and said unto her, Woman, thou art loosed from thine infirmity.

13 And he laid his hands on her: and immediately she was made straight, and glorified God.

Prayer:

Lord this sickness has plagued me for a long time but today as your child, I take deliverance from it all

Jesus Heals Man With Dropsy — Luke 14:1-4

1 And it came to pass, as he went into the house of one of the chief Pharisees to eat bread on the sabbath day, that they watched him.

2 And, behold, there was a certain man before him which had the dropsy.

3 And Jesus answering spake unto the lawyers and Pharisees, saying, Is it lawful to heal on the sabbath day?

4 And they held their peace. And he took him, and healed him, and let him go;

Prayer:

Jesus my healer, heal my infirmity and sickness as you did for the man with dropsy for you are the same today

Luke 17:11-17 — *Jesus Heals The Lepers*

11 And it came to pass, as he went to Jerusalem, that he passed through the midst of Samaria and Galilee.

12 And as he entered into a certain village, there met him ten men that were lepers, which stood afar off:

13 And they lifted up their voices, and said, Jesus, Master, have mercy on us.

14 And when he saw them, he said unto them, Go shew yourselves unto the priests. And it came to pass, that, as they went, they were cleansed.

15 And one of them, when he saw that he was healed, turned back, and with a loud voice glorified God,

16 And fell down on his face at his feet, giving him thanks: and he was a Samaritan.

17 And Jesus answering said, Were there not ten cleansed? but where are the nine?

contd.

Jesus Heals The Lepers — Luke 17:18-19

18 There are not found that returned to give glory to God, save this stranger.

19 And he said unto him, Arise, go thy way: thy faith hath made thee whole.

Prayer:

At your word dear Jesus, I receive my healing and I thank you for taking my sickness upon your own body

Luke 18:35-41 — *Jesus Heals The Blind Man*

35 And it came to pass, that as he was come nigh unto Jericho, a certain blind man sat by the way side begging:

36 And hearing the multitude pass by, he asked what it meant.

37 And they told him, that Jesus of Nazareth passeth by.

38 And he cried, saying, Jesus, thou son of David, have mercy on me.

39 And they which went before rebuked him, that he should hold his peace: but he cried so much the more, Thou son of David, have mercy on me.

40 And Jesus stood, and commanded him to be brought unto him: and when he was come near, he asked him,

41 Saying, What wilt thou that I shall do unto thee? And he said, Lord, that I may receive my sight.

contd.

Jesus Heals The Blind Man — Luke 18:42-43

42 And Jesus said unto him, Receive thy sight: thy faith hath saved thee.

43 And immediately he received his sight, and followed him, glorifying God: and all the people, when they saw it, gave praise unto God.

Prayer:

Lord I come to you that I may receive my healing from this my condition

Luke 22:31-32 — *I Have Prayed For You*

31 And the Lord said, Simon, Simon, behold, Satan hath desired to have you, that he may sift you as wheat:

32 But I have prayed for thee, that thy faith fail not: and when thou art converted, strengthen thy brethren.

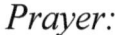

Prayer:

Thank you Lord Jesus for praying for me before you went to the cross; I am delivered from the power of the devil

Jesus Heals A Man's Ear — Luke 22:47-51

47 And while he yet spake, behold a multitude, and he that was called Judas, one of the twelve, went before them, and drew near unto Jesus to kiss him.

48 But Jesus said unto him, Judas, betrayest thou the Son of man with a kiss?

49 When they which were about him saw what would follow, they said unto him, Lord, shall we smite with the sword?

50 And one of them smote the servant of the high priest, and cut off his right ear.

51 And Jesus answered and said, Suffer ye thus far. And he touched his ear, and healed him.

Prayer:

Jesus Christ my Lord, I have suffered this wound, I receive your touch and healing on this wounded body

HEALINGS FROM THE BOOK OF
JOHN

Jesus Heals Nobleman's Son — John 4:46-51

46 So Jesus came again into Cana of Galilee, where he made the water wine. And there was a certain nobleman, whose son was sick at Capernaum.

47 When he heard that Jesus was come out of Judaea into Galilee, he went unto him, and besought him that he would come down, and heal his son: for he was at the point of death.

48 Then said Jesus unto him, Except ye see signs and wonders, ye will not believe.

49 The nobleman saith unto him, Sir, come down ere my child die.

50 Jesus saith unto him, Go thy way; thy son liveth. And the man believed the word that Jesus had spoken unto him, and he went his way.

51 And as he was now going down, his servants met him, and told him, saying, Thy son liveth.

contd.

John 4:52-53 — *Jesus Heals Nobleman's Son*

52 Then enquired he of them the hour when he began to amend. And they said unto him, Yesterday at the seventh hour the fever left him.

53 So the father knew that it was at the same hour, in the which Jesus said unto him, Thy son liveth: and himself believed, and his whole house.

Prayer:

O Lord God, I take your written word on healing in faith and I go my way because my body has begun to recover

Man By The Pool Of Bethesda   **John 5:1-6**

1 After this there was a feast of the Jews; and Jesus went up to Jerusalem.

2 Now there is at Jerusalem by the sheep market a pool, which is called in the Hebrew tongue Bethesda, having five porches.

3 In these lay a great multitude of impotent folk, of blind, halt, withered, waiting for the moving of the water.

4 For an angel went down at a certain season into the pool, and troubled the water: whosoever then first after the troubling of the water stepped in was made whole of whatsoever disease he had.

5 And a certain man was there, which had an infirmity thirty and eight years.

6 When Jesus saw him lie, and knew that he had been now a long time in that case, he saith unto him, Wilt thou be made whole?

contd.

John 5:7-9 *Man By The Pool of Bethesda*

7 The impotent man answered him, Sir, I have no man, when the water is troubled, to put me into the pool: but while I am coming, another steppeth down before me.

8 Jesus saith unto him, Rise, take up thy bed, and walk.

9 And immediately the man was made whole, and took up his bed, and walked: and on the same day was the sabbath.

Prayer:

Thank you Jesus for approaching me with your healing power; I obey your word and act accordingly

Jesus Heals The Blind Man — John 9:1-7

1 And as Jesus passed by, he saw a man which was blind from his birth.

2 And his disciples asked him, saying, Master, who did sin, this man, or his parents, that he was born blind?

3 Jesus answered, Neither hath this man sinned, nor his parents: but that the works of God should be made manifest in him.

4 I must work the works of him that sent me, while it is day: the night cometh, when no man can work.

5 As long as I am in the world, I am the light of the world.

6 When he had thus spoken, he spat on the ground, and made clay of the spittle, and he anointed the eyes of the blind man with the clay,

7 And said unto him, Go, wash in the pool of Siloam, (which is by interpretation, Sent.) He went his way therefore, and washed, and came seeing.

Prayer:

O Lord anoint my sick body with your clay that I may wash in the pool of your word and be restored

John 11:38-44 — Jesus Raises Lazarus

38 Jesus therefore again groaning in himself cometh to the grave. It was a cave, and a stone lay upon it.

39 Jesus said, Take ye away the stone. Martha, the sister of him that was dead, saith unto him, Lord, by this time he stinketh: for he hath been dead four days.

40 Jesus saith unto her, Said I not unto thee, that, if thou wouldest believe, thou shouldest see the glory of God?

41 Then they took away the stone from the place where the dead was laid. And Jesus lifted up his eyes, and said, Father, I thank thee that thou hast heard me.

42 And I knew that thou hearest me always: but because of the people which stand by I said it, that they may believe that thou hast sent me.

43 And when he thus had spoken, he cried with a loud voice, Lazarus, come forth.

44 And he that was dead came forth, bound hand and foot with graveclothes: and his face was bound about with a napkin. Jesus saith unto them, Loose him, and let him go.

Prayer:

Father, I roll away the stone of infirmity, sickness and death; I take healing from your word; I let go all weights

# HEALINGS FROM THE BOOK OF

ACTS

He Shewed Himself Alive — Acts 1:1-3

1 The former treatise have I made, O Theophilus, of all that Jesus began both to do and teach,

2 Until the day in which he was taken up, after that he through the Holy Ghost had given commandments unto the apostles whom he had chosen:

3 To whom also he shewed himself alive after his passion by many infallible proofs, being seen of them forty days, and speaking of the things pertaining to the kingdom of God:

Prayer:

Lord Jesus you died and rose that I may live, I therefore receive your life in my body in the name of Jesus

Acts 3:1-8 — *Healing At The Beautiful Gate*

1 Now Peter and John went up together into the temple at the hour of prayer, being the ninth hour.

2 And a certain man lame from his mother's womb was carried, whom they laid daily at the gate of the temple which is called Beautiful, to ask alms of them that entered into the temple;

3 Who seeing Peter and John about to go into the temple asked an alms.

4 And Peter, fastening his eyes upon him with John, said, Look on us.

5 And he gave heed unto them, expecting to receive something of them.

6 Then Peter said, Silver and gold have I none; but such as I have give I thee: In the name of Jesus Christ of Nazareth rise up and walk.

7 And he took him by the right hand, and lifted him up: and immediately his feet and ankle bones received strength.

8 And he leaping up stood, and walked, and entered with them into the temple, walking, and leaping, and praising God.

contd.

Healing At The Beautiful Gate   **Acts 3:9-10**

9 And all the people saw him walking and praising God:

10 And they knew that it was he which sat for alms at the Beautiful gate of the temple: and they were filled with wonder and amazement at that which had happened unto him.

Prayer:

Through faith in the name of Jesus Christ of Nazareth, my body I command you, function as God created you to

Acts 5:15-16 — *The Shadow Of Peter Heals The Sick*

15 Insomuch that they brought forth the sick into the streets, and laid them on beds and couches, that at the least the shadow of Peter passing by might overshadow some of them.

16 There came also a multitude out of the cities round about unto Jerusalem, bringing sick folks, and them which were vexed with unclean spirits: and they were healed every one.

Prayer:

Lord I release my faith in your word to receive healing from the Church elder's anointing

Philip's Miracles In Samaria — Acts 8:5-8

5 Then Philip went down to the city of Samaria, and preached Christ unto them.

6 And the people with one accord gave heed unto those things which Philip spake, hearing and seeing the miracles which he did.

7 For unclean spirits, crying with loud voice, came out of many that were possessed with them: and many taken with palsies, and that were lame, were healed.

8 And there was great joy in that city.

Prayer:

Lord as I hear, study and meditate on your word, may every unclean spirit flee from my body, finance and life

Acts 8:12-13 — *Philip's Preaching And Miracles*

12 But when they believed Philip preaching the things concerning the kingdom of God, and the name of Jesus Christ, they were baptized, both men and women.

13 Then Simon himself believed also: and when he was baptized, he continued with Philip, and wondered, beholding the miracles and signs which were done.

Prayer:

Father, as I behold the miracles and signs done by your servant, may I be a partaker also

Peter Heals Man With Palsy — Acts 9:32-35

32 And it came to pass, as Peter passed throughout all quarters, he came down also to the saints which dwelt at Lydda.

33 And there he found a certain man named Aeneas, which had kept his bed eight years, and was sick of the palsy.

34 And Peter said unto him, Aeneas, Jesus Christ maketh thee whole: arise, and make thy bed. And he arose immediately.

35 And all that dwelt at Lydda and Saron saw him, and turned to the Lord.

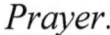

Prayer:

Dear Lord, I have been afflicted for a very long time, but today I receive healing and wholeness from you Jesus

Acts 9:36-40 — Peter Raises The Dead

36 Now there was at Joppa a certain disciple named Tabitha, which by interpretation is called Dorcas: this woman was full of good works and almsdeeds which she did.

37 And it came to pass in those days, that she was sick, and died: whom when they had washed, they laid her in an upper chamber.

38 And forasmuch as Lydda was nigh to Joppa, and the disciples had heard that Peter was there, they sent unto him two men, desiring him that he would not delay to come to them.

39 Then Peter arose and went with them. When he was come, they brought him into the upper chamber: and all the widows stood by him weeping, and shewing the coats and garments which Dorcas made, while she was with them.

40 But Peter put them all forth, and kneeled down, and prayed; and turning him to the body said, Tabitha, arise. And she opened her eyes: and when she saw Peter, she sat up.

contd.

Peter Raises The Dead   Acts 9:41-42

41 And he gave her his hand, and lifted her up, and when he had called the saints and widows, presented her alive.

42 And it was known throughout all Joppa; and many believed in the Lord.

Prayer:

Lord, kindness may get your attention, yet by grace through faith I claim healing and the dead raised to life

Acts 14:6-10 — *Peter Heals Man With Palsy*

6 They were ware of it, and fled unto Lystra and Derbe, cities of Lycaonia, and unto the region that lieth round about:

7 And there they preached the gospel.

8 And there sat a certain man at Lystra, impotent in his feet, being a cripple from his mother's womb, who never had walked:

9 The same heard Paul speak: who stedfastly beholding him, and perceiving that he had faith to be healed,

10 Said with a loud voice, Stand upright on thy feet. And he leaped and walked.

Prayer:

Father, as I continue to hear and read your word, as my faith grows, may my healing be perfected as I obey

The Possessed Damsel — Acts 16:14-18

14 And a certain woman named Lydia, a seller of purple, of the city of Thyatira, which worshipped God, heard us: whose heart the Lord opened, that she attended unto the things which were spoken of Paul.

15 And when she was baptized, and her household, she besought us, saying, If ye have judged me to be faithful to the Lord, come into my house, and abide there. And she constrained us.

16 And it came to pass, as we went to prayer, a certain damsel possessed with a spirit of divination met us, which brought her masters much gain by soothsaying:

17 The same followed Paul and us, and cried, saying, These men are the servants of the most high God, which shew unto us the way of salvation.

18 And this did she many days. But Paul, being grieved, turned and said to the spirit, I command thee in the name of Jesus Christ to come out of her. And he came out the same hour.

Prayer:

You spirit of sickness, disease and infirmity I command you in the name of Jesus Christ to come out of me!

Acts 19:11-12   *Paul Heals With Handkerchiefs*

11 And God wrought special miracles by the hands of Paul:

12 So that from his body were brought unto the sick handkerchiefs or aprons, and the diseases departed from them, and the evil spirits went out of them.

Prayer:

O Lord, as I touch this cloth prayed upon by your servant, just like Paul, may devils and sicknesses flee

Paul Brings Young Man To Life   Acts 20:8-12

8 And there were many lights in the upper chamber, where they were gathered together.

9 And there sat in a window a certain young man named Eutychus, being fallen into a deep sleep: and as Paul was long preaching, he sunk down with sleep, and fell down from the third loft, and was taken up dead.

10 And Paul went down, and fell on him, and embracing him said, Trouble not yourselves; for his life is in him.

11 When he therefore was come up again, and had broken bread, and eaten, and talked a long while, even till break of day, so he departed.

12 And they brought the young man alive, and were not a little comforted.

Prayer:

*As an heir to the promise in Christ,
I ask O Lord that as I pray for the dead,
you will raise them as promised*

Acts 28:1-6 — *Paul Shook Off The Beast*

1 And when they were escaped, then they knew that the island was called Melita.

2 And the barbarous people shewed us no little kindness: for they kindled a fire, and received us every one, because of the present rain, and because of the cold.

3 And when Paul had gathered a bundle of sticks, and laid them on the fire, there came a viper out of the heat, and fastened on his hand.

4 And when the barbarians saw the venomous beast hang on his hand, they said among themselves, No doubt this man is a murderer, whom, though he hath escaped the sea, yet vengeance suffereth not to live.

5 And he shook off the beast into the fire, and felt no harm.

6 Howbeit they looked when he should have swollen, or fallen down dead suddenly: but after they had looked a great while, and saw no harm come to him, they changed their minds, and said that he was a god.

Prayer:

No weapon formed against me shall prosper so I shake off every attack of the devil into the fire

Peter Heals Publius's Father — Acts 28:8-9

8 And it came to pass, that the father of Publius lay sick of a fever and of a bloody flux: to whom Paul entered in, and prayed, and laid his hands on him, and healed him.

9 So when this was done, others also, which had diseases in the island, came, and were healed

Prayer:

As I lay my hands on this sick part of my body, I speak healing and command the spirit responsible to flee

HEALINGS FROM THE BOOK OF
ROMANS

God Quickens Your Mortal Body   **Romans 8:9-11**

9 But ye are not in the flesh, but in the Spirit, if so be that the Spirit of God dwell in you. Now if any man have not the Spirit of Christ, he is none of his.

10 And if Christ be in you, the body is dead because of sin; but the Spirit is life because of righteousness.

11 But if the Spirit of him that raised up Jesus from the dead dwell in you, he that raised up Christ from the dead shall also quicken your mortal bodies by his Spirit that dwelleth in you.

Prayer:

Thank you Jesus for as I acknowledge this truth, the life of the spirit will surely manifest in every part of my body

Romans 15:18-19 — *Mighty Signs And Wonders*

18 For I will not dare to speak of any of those things which Christ hath not wrought by me, to make the Gentiles obedient, by word and deed,

19 Through mighty signs and wonders, by the power of the Spirit of God; so that from Jerusalem, and round about unto Illyricum, I have fully preached the gospel of Christ.

Prayer:

As I preach the gospel, I receive signs and wonders in my life as well as the lives of those who will hear

HEALINGS FROM THE BOOK OF
1 CORINTHIANS

God Makes Way Of Escape — 1 Corinthians 10:11-13

11 Now all these things happened unto them for examples: and they are written for our admonition, upon whom the ends of the world are come.

12 Wherefore let him that thinketh he standeth take heed lest he fall.

13 There hath no temptation taken you but such as is common to man: but God is faithful, who will not suffer you to be tempted above that ye are able; but will with the temptation also make a way to escape, that ye may be able to bear it.

Prayer:

Faithful God, I have suffered this temptation for long, I ask for grace to bear and direction to escape

1 Corinthians 12:7-9

The Gifts Of Healing

7 But the manifestation of the Spirit is given to every man to profit withal.

8 For to one is given by the Spirit the word of wisdom; to another the word of knowledge by the same Spirit;

9 To another faith by the same Spirit; to another the gifts of healing by the same Spirit;

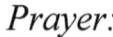

Prayer:

Thank you God for the gift of healing given to the Church, help me partake of this gift that I may be healed

The Gifts Of Healing   1 Corinthians 12:25-30

25 That there should be no schism in the body; but that the members should have the same care one for another.

26 And whether one member suffer, all the members suffer with it; or one member be honoured, all the members rejoice with it.

27 Now ye are the body of Christ, and members in particular.

28 And God hath set some in the church, first apostles, secondarily prophets, thirdly teachers, after that miracles, then gifts of healings, helps, governments, diversities of tongues.

29 Are all apostles? are all prophets? are all teachers? are all workers of miracles?

30 Have all the gifts of healing? do all speak with tongues? do all interpret?

Prayer:

Lord may those in your body with the gift of healing use it in love by your Spirit to benefit your church

HEALINGS FROM THE BOOK OF
2 CORINTHIANS

Our Bodies God's Temple — 2 Corinthians 6:15-16

15 And what concord hath Christ with Belial? or what part hath he that believeth with an infidel?

16 And what agreement hath the temple of God with idols? for ye are the temple of the living God; as God hath said, I will dwell in them, and walk in them; and I will be their God, and they shall be my people.

Prayer:

My body which is God's temple has no agreement with idols, my body will not act in agreement with sickness

2 Corinthians 7:1   *Filthiness Of The Flesh*

1 Having therefore these promises, dearly beloved, let us cleanse ourselves from all filthiness of the flesh and spirit, perfecting holiness in the fear of God.

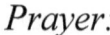

Prayer:

In the name of Jesus, I refuse to give place to any filthiness of the flesh in the form of sin or sickness

HEALINGS FROM THE BOOK OF
GALATIANS

Redeemed From The Curse   **Galatians 3:11-14**

11 But that no man is justified by the law in the sight of God, it is evident: for, The just shall live by faith.

12 And the law is not of faith: but, The man that doeth them shall live in them.

13 Christ hath redeemed us from the curse of the law, being made a curse for us: for it is written, Cursed is every one that hangeth on a tree:

14 That the blessing of Abraham might come on the Gentiles through Jesus Christ; that we might receive the promise of the Spirit through faith.

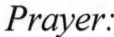

Prayer:

Thank you Jesus for redeeming me from the curse of the law; this means sickness no longer has authority over me

Galatians 2:19-20   *I Live By The Faith Of Jesus*

19 For I through the law am dead to the law, that I might live unto God.

20 I am crucified with Christ: nevertheless I live; yet not I, but Christ liveth in me: and the life which I now live in the flesh I live by the faith of the Son of God, who loved me, and gave himself for me.

Prayer:

I declare, the life which I now live in my body I live by the faith of Jesus in health, strength and sound mind

Stand Fast In Christ's Liberty   **Galatians 5:1-2**

1 Stand fast therefore in the liberty wherewith Christ hath made us free, and be not entangled again with the yoke of bondage.

2 Behold, I Paul say unto you, that if ye be circumcised, Christ shall profit you nothing.

Prayer:

Sin and sickness are yoke, I resist the yoke of the devil and stand fast in my freedom of healing and health

HEALINGS FROM THE BOOK OF
EPHESIANS

Blessed With All Spiritual Blessings   **Ephesians 1:2-3**

2 Grace be to you, and peace, from God our Father, and from the Lord Jesus Christ.

3 Blessed be the God and Father of our Lord Jesus Christ, who hath blessed us with all spiritual blessings in heavenly places in Christ:

Prayer:

I thank you O God for blessing me with all spiritual blessings which includes health; I take my healing now

Ephesians 1:6-7 *Redemption Through His Blood*

6 To the praise of the glory of his grace, wherein he hath made us accepted in the beloved.

7 In whom we have redemption through his blood, the forgiveness of sins, according to the riches of his grace;

Prayer:

Lord, I have redemption and forgiveness of sins through your blood, hence I refuse to give place to sickness

God's Power Towards Believers — Ephesians 1:15-21

15 Wherefore I also, after I heard of your faith in the Lord Jesus, and love unto all the saints,

16 Cease not to give thanks for you, making mention of you in my prayers;

17 That the God of our Lord Jesus Christ, the Father of glory, may give unto you the spirit of wisdom and revelation in the knowledge of him:

18 The eyes of your understanding being enlightened; that ye may know what is the hope of his calling, and what the riches of the glory of his inheritance in the saints,

19 And what is the exceeding greatness of his power to us-ward who believe, according to the working of his mighty power,

20 Which he wrought in Christ, when he raised him from the dead, and set him at his own right hand in the heavenly places,

21 Far above all principality, and power, and might, and dominion, and every name that is named, not only in this world, but also in that which is to come:

Prayer:

Healing is in the riches of the glory of your inheritance; with your power in me, I rebuke all sickness and devils

Ephesians 2:4-6 *God Quickened Believers*

4 But God, who is rich in mercy, for his great love wherewith he loved us,

5 Even when we were dead in sins, hath quickened us together with Christ, (by grace ye are saved;)

6 And hath raised us up together, and made us sit together in heavenly places in Christ Jesus:

Prayer:

Thank you Father for quickening me with Christ; now my body I command you, respond to the life of Christ in you!

God Is Able To Do More — Ephesians 3:14-20

14 For this cause I bow my knees unto the Father of our Lord Jesus Christ,

15 Of whom the whole family in heaven and earth is named,

16 That he would grant you, according to the riches of his glory, to be strengthened with might by his Spirit in the inner man;

17 That Christ may dwell in your hearts by faith; that ye, being rooted and grounded in love,

18 May be able to comprehend with all saints what is the breadth, and length, and depth, and height;

19 And to know the love of Christ, which passeth knowledge, that ye might be filled with all the fulness of God.

20 Now unto him that is able to do exceeding abundantly above all that we ask or think, according to the power that worketh in us,

Prayer:

Lord, I receive strength with might by your Spirit in my inner man, and healing according to your power in me

Ephesians 6:10-17 — *The Whole Armour Of God*

10 Finally, my brethren, be strong in the Lord, and in the power of his might.

11 Put on the whole armour of God, that ye may be able to stand against the wiles of the devil.

12 For we wrestle not against flesh and blood, but against principalities, against powers, against the rulers of the darkness of this world, against spiritual wickedness in high places.

13 Wherefore take unto you the whole armour of God, that ye may be able to withstand in the evil day, and having done all, to stand.

14 Stand therefore, having your loins girt about with truth, and having on the breastplate of righteousness;

15 And your feet shod with the preparation of the gospel of peace;

16 Above all, taking the shield of faith, wherewith ye shall be able to quench all the fiery darts of the wicked.

17 And take the helmet of salvation, and the sword of the Spirit, which is the word of God:

contd.

The Whole Armour Of God — Ephesians 6:18

18 Praying always with all prayer and supplication in the Spirit, and watching; thereunto with all perseverance and supplication for all saints;

Prayer:

Father I thank you; with my shield of faith I resist the lies of the devil and with the word I rebuke all sicknesses

HEALINGS FROM THE BOOK OF
PHILIPPIANS

Every Knee Shall Bow — Philippians 2:8-10

8 And being found in fashion as a man, he humbled himself, and became obedient unto death, even the death of the cross.

9 Wherefore God also hath highly exalted him, and given him a name which is above every name:

10 That at the name of Jesus every knee should bow, of things in heaven, and things in earth, and things under the earth;

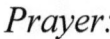

Prayer:

At the name of Jesus every knee bows; I command sickness and devils to leave my body in Jesus name!

Philippians 2:25-27

God Heals Epaphroditus

25 Yet I supposed it necessary to send to you Epaphroditus, my brother, and companion in labour, and fellowsoldier, but your messenger, and he that ministered to my wants.

26 For he longed after you all, and was full of heaviness, because that ye had heard that he had been sick.

27 For indeed he was sick nigh unto death: but God had mercy on him; and not on him only, but on me also, lest I should have sorrow upon sorrow.

Prayer:

Father, in your mercy heal me for you promised to satisfy me with long life as your child and servant

Be Careful For Nothing — Philippians 4:6-7

6 Be careful for nothing; but in every thing by prayer and supplication with thanksgiving let your requests be made known unto God.

7 And the peace of God, which passeth all understanding, shall keep your hearts and minds through Christ Jesus.

Prayer:

Dear God, I feel anxious but you said I should not, so I come to you in prayer and thanksgiving to receive peace

HEALINGS FROM THE BOOK OF COLOSSIANS

God Delivered Us — Colossians 1:12-14

12 Giving thanks unto the Father, which hath made us meet to be partakers of the inheritance of the saints in light:

13 Who hath delivered us from the power of darkness, and hath translated us into the kingdom of his dear Son:

14 In whom we have redemption through his blood, even the forgiveness of sins:

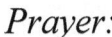

Prayer:

O merciful Lord, thank you for delivering me from the power of darkness by redemption from sin and sickness

Colossians 2:14-15   *Jesus Spoiled Principalities*

14 Blotting out the handwriting of ordinances that was against us, which was contrary to us, and took it out of the way, nailing it to his cross;

15 And having spoiled principalities and powers, he made a shew of them openly, triumphing over them in it.

Prayer:

I take my healing by faith in your word, for you O God have spoiled principalities of sickness, disease and death

HEALINGS FROM THE BOOK OF
1 THESSALONIANS

Whole Body Be Blameless — 1 Thessalonians 5:20-23

20 Despise not prophesyings.

21 Prove all things; hold fast that which is good.

22 Abstain from all appearance of evil.

23 And the very God of peace sanctify you wholly; and I pray God your whole spirit and soul and body be preserved blameless unto the coming of our Lord Jesus Christ.

Prayer:

By the power of the Holy Spirit, my spirit soul and body will be preserved in health and sound mind

HEALINGS FROM THE BOOK OF
2 THESSALONIANS

God Keeps From All Evil — 2 Thessalonians 3:1-3

1 Finally, brethren, pray for us, that the word of the Lord may have free course, and be glorified, even as it is with you:

2 And that we may be delivered from unreasonable and wicked men: for all men have not faith.

3 But the Lord is faithful, who shall stablish you, and keep you from evil.

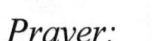

Prayer:

Faithful Father, you promised to keep me from evil; I therefore resist all evil and receive divine establishment

HEALINGS FROM THE BOOK OF
1 TIMOTHY

Bodily Exercise Profiteth Little 1 Timothy 4:8-9

8 For bodily exercise profiteth little: but godliness is profitable unto all things, having promise of the life that now is, and of that which is to come.

9 This is a faithful saying and worthy of all acceptation.

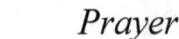

Prayer:

Grant me grace not to neglect my body by exercising it for health, even as my spirit is exercised in righteousness

1 Timothy 5:22-23 — *A Little Wine For Stomach*

22 Lay hands suddenly on no man, neither be partaker of other men's sins: keep thyself pure.

23 Drink no longer water, but use a little wine for thy stomach's sake and thine often infirmities

Prayer:

Father, give me wisdom to keep from sin as I seek the elders in the church to lay hand on me for healing

HEALINGS FROM THE BOOK OF
2 TIMOTHY

Spirit Of Power Love And Sound Mind   **2 Timothy 1:6-7**

6 Wherefore I put thee in remembrance that thou stir up the gift of God, which is in thee by the putting on of my hands.

7 For God hath not given us the spirit of fear; but of power, and of love, and of a sound mind.

Prayer:

Thank you Lord for you have not given me a spirit of fear therefore in boldness, I cast down every thought of fear

2 Timothy 4:17-18 — *The Lord Shall Deliver Me*

17 Notwithstanding the Lord stood with me, and strengthened me; that by me the preaching might be fully known, and that all the Gentiles might hear: and I was delivered out of the mouth of the lion.

18 And the Lord shall deliver me from every evil work, and will preserve me unto his heavenly kingdom: to whom be glory for ever and ever. Amen.

Prayer:

Dear God, I receive deliverance from every evil work, and preservation unto health, long life and prosperity

HEALINGS FROM THE BOOK OF
TITUS

The Washing Of Regeneration — **Titus 3:3-5**

3 For we ourselves also were sometimes foolish, disobedient, deceived, serving divers lusts and pleasures, living in malice and envy, hateful, and hating one another.

4 But after that the kindness and love of God our Saviour toward man appeared,

5 Not by works of righteousness which we have done, but according to his mercy he saved us, by the washing of regeneration, and renewing of the Holy Ghost;

Prayer:

I lived in disobedience but Lord in your mercy, you saved me renewing my spirit and body, healing all my diseases

HEALINGS FROM THE BOOK OF
PHILEMON

Effectual Communication Of Faith — Philemon 1:4-6

4 I thank my God, making mention of thee always in my prayers,

5 Hearing of thy love and faith, which thou hast toward the Lord Jesus, and toward all saints;

6 That the communication of thy faith may become effectual by the acknowledging of every good thing which is in you in Christ Jesus.

Prayer:

Lord help me acknowledge every good thing in me to effectively communicate my faith against all sicknesses

HEALINGS FROM THE BOOK OF
HEBREW

Jesus Delivers From Fear — Hebrews 2:11-15

11 For both he that sanctifieth and they who are sanctified are all of one: for which cause he is not ashamed to call them brethren,

12 Saying, I will declare thy name unto my brethren, in the midst of the church will I sing praise unto thee.

13 And again, I will put my trust in him. And again, Behold I and the children which God hath given me.

14 Forasmuch then as the children are partakers of flesh and blood, he also himself likewise took part of the same; that through death he might destroy him that had the power of death, that is, the devil;

15 And deliver them who through fear of death were all their lifetime subject to bondage.

Prayer:

Thank you Father for delivering me from bondage; I take authority over the destroyed devil, sickness and diseases

Hebrews 4:9-12 — *The Word Is Quick, And Powerful*

9 There remaineth therefore a rest to the people of God.

10 For he that is entered into his rest, he also hath ceased from his own works, as God did from his.

11 Let us labour therefore to enter into that rest, lest any man fall after the same example of unbelief.

12 For the word of God is quick, and powerful, and sharper than any twoedged sword, piercing even to the dividing asunder of soul and spirit, and of the joints and marrow, and is a discerner of the thoughts and intents of the heart.

Prayer:

Father with your sword I pull down the works of the devil in my thoughts and body and enter into your rest

Let Us Hold Fast Our Profession   Hebrews 4:14-16

14 Seeing then that we have a great high priest, that is passed into the heavens, Jesus the Son of God, let us hold fast our profession.

15 For we have not an high priest which cannot be touched with the feeling of our infirmities; but was in all points tempted like as we are, yet without sin.

16 Let us therefore come boldly unto the throne of grace, that we may obtain mercy, and find grace to help in time of need.

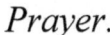

Prayer:

Thank you Lord, by the stripes of Jesus I was healed therefore I am well; I hold fast to this confession

Hebrews 10:21-23   *Let Us Hold Fast The Profession*

21 And having an high priest over the house of God;

22 Let us draw near with a true heart in full assurance of faith, having our hearts sprinkled from an evil conscience, and our bodies washed with pure water.

23 Let us hold fast the profession of our faith without wavering; (for he is faithful that promised;)

Prayer:

Lord I draw near with a true heart in full assurance of faith, to receive my healing from my high priest Jesus

The Just Shall Live By Faith   **Hebrews 10:35-39**

35 Cast not away therefore your confidence, which hath great recompence of reward.

36 For ye have need of patience, that, after ye have done the will of God, ye might receive the promise.

37 For yet a little while, and he that shall come will come, and will not tarry.

38 Now the just shall live by faith: but if any man draw back, my soul shall have no pleasure in him.

39 But we are not of them who draw back unto perdition; but of them that believe to the saving of the soul.

Prayer:

Though I may not see a physical manifestation yet, Lord I hold fast to my healing in full confidence and faith

Hebrews 11:1-6 — *What Faith Is*

1 Now faith is the substance of things hoped for, the evidence of things not seen.

2 For by it the elders obtained a good report.

3 Through faith we understand that the worlds were framed by the word of God, so that things which are seen were not made of things which do appear.

4 By faith Abel offered unto God a more excellent sacrifice than Cain, by which he obtained witness that he was righteous, God testifying of his gifts: and by it he being dead yet speaketh.

5 By faith Enoch was translated that he should not see death; and was not found, because God had translated him: for before his translation he had this testimony, that he pleased God.

6 But without faith it is impossible to please him: for he that cometh to God must believe that he is, and that he is a rewarder of them that diligently seek him.

Prayer:

Lord, I believe I received my healing when I prayed even if it is not yet visible; my faith is giving substance to it

But Let It Rather Be Healed   Hebrews 12:12-14

12 Wherefore lift up the hands which hang down, and the feeble knees;

13 And make straight paths for your feet, lest that which is lame be turned out of the way; but let it rather be healed.

14 Follow peace with all men, and holiness, without which no man shall see the Lord:

Prayer:

Dear Jesus, I refuse to stay passive in sickness; I take action in your word and receive healing in my body

Hebrews 13:5-6 *I Will Never Leave Thee*

5 Let your conversation be without covetousness; and be content with such things as ye have: for he hath said, I will never leave thee, nor forsake thee.

6 So that we may boldly say, The Lord is my helper, and I will not fear what man shall do unto me.

Prayer:

Father, I boldly say, you are my helper in healing and health, and I will not be afraid for greater is Jesus in me

Jesus Christ The Same   Hebrews 13:8-9

8 Jesus Christ the same yesterday, and to day, and for ever.

9 Be not carried about with divers and strange doctrines. For it is a good thing that the heart be established with grace; not with meats, which have not profited them that have been occupied therein.

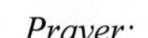

Prayer:

Lord Jesus, you heal and raise the dead today as in days of old for you are the same yesterday, today and forever

HEALINGS FROM THE BOOK OF
JAMES

Ask In Faith, Nothing Wavering — James 1:6-8

6 But let him ask in faith, nothing wavering. For he that wavereth is like a wave of the sea driven with the wind and tossed.

7 For let not that man think that he shall receive any thing of the Lord.

8 A double minded man is unstable in all his ways

Prayer:

Dear Father, I have asked for healing in faith, help me to stay in your word so that I would not waver

James 2:14-22 — *Faith With Works*

14 What doth it profit, my brethren, though a man say he hath faith, and have not works? can faith save him?

15 If a brother or sister be naked, and destitute of daily food,

16 And one of you say unto them, Depart in peace, be ye warmed and filled; notwithstanding ye give them not those things which are needful to the body; what doth it profit?

17 Even so faith, if it hath not works, is dead, being alone.

18 Yea, a man may say, Thou hast faith, and I have works: shew me thy faith without thy works, and I will shew thee my faith by my works.

19 Thou believest that there is one God; thou doest well: the devils also believe, and tremble.

20 But wilt thou know, O vain man, that faith without works is dead?

21 Was not Abraham our father justified by works, when he had offered Isaac his son upon the altar?

22 Seest thou how faith wrought with his works, and by works was faith made perfect?

contd.

Faith With Works   **James 2:23-24**

23 And the scripture was fulfilled which saith, Abraham believed God, and it was imputed unto him for righteousness: and he was called the Friend of God.

24 Ye see then how that by works a man is justified, and not by faith only.

Prayer:

Thank you Lord for healing me as I prayed in faith, help me stay in your word to live the works of my faith

James 4:7-8 — *Resist The Devil*

7 Submit yourselves therefore to God. Resist the devil, and he will flee from you.

8 Draw nigh To God, and he will draw nigh to you. Cleanse your hands, ye sinners; and purify your hearts, ye double minded.

Prayer:

By the stripes of Jesus I was healed; these symptoms are lies of the devil – I therefore resist you lying symptoms

Prayer Of Faith Shall Save The Sick   **James 5:13-16**

13 Is any among you afflicted? let him pray. Is any merry? let him sing psalms.

14 Is any sick among you? let him call for the elders of the church; and let them pray over him, anointing him with oil in the name of the Lord:

15 And the prayer of faith shall save the sick, and the Lord shall raise him up; and if he have committed sins, they shall be forgiven him.

16 Confess your faults one to another, and pray one for another, that ye may be healed. The effectual fervent prayer of a righteous man availeth much.

Prayer:

O Lord I receive my healing as the elders of the church pray over me, anointing me with oil in the name of Jesus

HEALINGS FROM THE BOOK OF
1 PETER

Kept By The Power Of God *1 Peter 1:3-5*

3 Blessed be the God and Father of our Lord Jesus Christ, which according to his abundant mercy hath begotten us again unto a lively hope by the resurrection of Jesus Christ from the dead,

4 To an inheritance incorruptible, and undefiled, and that fadeth not away, reserved in heaven for you,

5 Who are kept by the power of God through faith unto salvation ready to be revealed in the last time.

Prayer:

I thank you O Father that my body is kept in health by the power of God through faith unto salvation

1 Peter 2:23-24   *By Whose Stripes Ye Were Healed*

23 Who, when he was reviled, reviled not again; when he suffered, he threatened not; but committed himself to him that judgeth righteously:

24 Who his own self bare our sins in his own body on the tree, that we, being dead to sins, should live unto righteousness: by whose stripes ye were healed.

Prayer:

Jesus I thank you for you bare my sins and sicknesses in your body on the tree and by your stripes I was healed

Love Life, And See Good Days — **1 Peter 3:9-12**

9 Not rendering evil for evil, or railing for railing: but contrariwise blessing; knowing that ye are thereunto called, that ye should inherit a blessing.

10 For he that will love life, and see good days, let him refrain his tongue from evil, and his lips that they speak no guile:

11 Let him eschew evil, and do good; let him seek peace, and ensue it.

12 For the eyes of the Lord are over the righteous, and his ears are open unto their prayers: but the face of the Lord is against them that do evil.

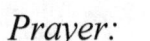

Prayer:

Your ears O God are open unto my prayers; your face is against them that do evil, deliver me from this affliction

1 Peter 5:7-9 *Whom Resist Stedfast In The Faith*

7 Casting all your care upon him; for he careth for you.

8 Be sober, be vigilant; because your adversary the devil, as a roaring lion, walketh about, seeking: whom he may devour

9 Whom resist stedfast in the faith, knowing that the same afflictions are accomplished in your brethren that are in the world.

Prayer:

Jesus I believe by your stripes I was healed, I steadfastly resist these lying symptoms and refuse to give in!

HEALINGS FROM THE BOOK OF
2 PETER

Given All That Pertain Unto Life   **2 Peter 1:2-4**

2 Grace and peace be multiplied unto you through the knowledge of God, and of Jesus our Lord,

3 According as his divine power hath given unto us all things that pertain unto life and godliness, through the knowledge of him that hath called us to glory and virtue:

4 Whereby are given unto us exceeding great and precious promises: that by these ye might be partakers of the divine nature, having escaped the corruption that is in the world through lust.

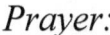

Prayer:

Father you have given me all things that pertain to life such as your divine nature; I therefore resist sickness

2 Peter 3:8-9 — *Thousand Years As One Day*

8 But, beloved, be not ignorant of this one thing, that one day is with the Lord as a thousand years, and a thousand years as one day.

9 The Lord is not slack concerning his promise, as some men count slackness; but is longsuffering to us-ward, not willing that any should perish, but that all should come to repentance.

Prayer:

Lord thank you for healing me by your stripes. I wait patiently in faith for a manifestation and I resist the devil

HEALINGS FROM THE BOOK OF
1 JOHN

Greater Is He That Is In You   **1 John 4:3-4**

3 And every spirit that confesseth not that Jesus Christ is come in the flesh is not of God: and this is that spirit of antichrist, whereof ye have heard that it should come; and even now already is it in the world.

4 Ye are of God, little children, and have overcome them: because greater is he that is in you, than he that is in the world.

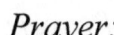

Prayer:

I command sickness, disease and pain to leave my body, for greater is he that is in me, than he that is in the world

1 John 5:4-5 *Victory That Overcometh The World*

4 For whatsoever is born of God overcometh the world: and this is the victory that overcometh the world, even our faith.

5 Who is he that overcometh the world, but he that believeth that Jesus is the Son of God?

Prayer:

Lord, you said whatsoever is born of God overcomes the world by faith; I therefore claim victory over sicknesses

We Have The Petitions   **1 John 5:14-15**

14 And this is the confidence that we have in him, that, if we ask any thing according to his will, he heareth us:

15 And if we know that he hear us, whatsoever we ask, we know that we have the petitions that we desired of him.

Prayer:

Health is your will Lord, I know you heard my request for healing; thank you I know I have my desired request

HEALINGS FROM THE BOOK OF
2 JOHN

Walk After His Commandments — 2 John 1:6

6 And this is love, that we walk after his commandments. This is the commandment, That, as ye have heard from the beginning, ye should walk in it.

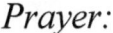

Prayer:

Thank you Lord, as when I walk in your commandment of love you keep me in health as I give the devil no foothold

HEALINGS FROM THE BOOK OF
3 JOHN

Prosper And Be In Health — 3 John 1:1-3

1 The elder unto the wellbeloved Gaius, whom I love in the truth.

2 Beloved, I wish above all things that thou mayest prosper and be in health, even as thy soul prospereth.

3 For I rejoiced greatly, when the brethren came and testified of the truth that is in thee, even as thou walkest in the truth.

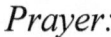

Prayer:

Thy will be done in my life O Lord, for you wish above all things that I prosper and be in health as my soul does

HEALINGS FROM THE BOOK OF
JUDE

Building Up Yourselves — **Jude 1:20-22**

20 But ye, beloved, building up yourselves on your most holy faith, praying in the Holy Ghost,

21 Keep yourselves in the love of God, looking for the mercy of our Lord Jesus Christ unto eternal life.

22 And of some have compassion, making a difference:

Prayer:

Dear Holy Spirit, help me build up my spirit, mind and body in my most holy faith, praying in the Holy Ghost

HEALINGS FROM THE BOOK OF
REVELATION

Healing Of The Nations — Revelation 22:2

2 In the midst of the street of it, and on either side of the river, was there the tree of life, which bare twelve manner of fruits, and yielded her fruit every month: and the leaves of the tree were for the healing of the nations.

Prayer:

Dear Lord Jesus who heals the nations,
I come to you with thanksgiving
to take the healing you have provided

SHORT VERSES ON
HEALING
FAITH
REBUKING THE DEVIL
PATIENCE

SHORT VERSES ON HEALING

Exodus 15:26b   I will put none of these diseases upon thee, which I have brought upon the Egyptians: for I am the Lord that healeth thee.

Exodus 23:25   And ye shall serve the Lord your God, and he shall bless thy bread, and thy water; and I will take sickness away from the midst of thee.

Exodus 23:26   There shall nothing cast their young, nor be barren, in thy land: the number of thy days I will fulfil.

Deuteronomy 7:15   And the Lord will take away from thee all sickness, and will put none of the evil diseases of Egypt, which thou knowest, upon thee; but will lay them upon all them that hate thee.

2 Kings 20:5b   I have heard thy prayer, I have seen thy tears: behold, I will heal thee: on the third day thou shalt go up unto the house of the LORD.

Isaiah 38:16   O Lord, by these things men live, and in all these things is the life of my spirit: so wilt thou recover me, and make me to live.

Isaiah 53:4-5   Surely he hath borne our griefs, and carried our sorrows: yet we did esteem him stricken, smitten of God, and afflicted. [5] But he was wounded for our transgressions, he was bruised for our iniquities: the chastisement of our peace was upon him; and with his stripes we are healed.

Isaiah 54:17   No weapon that is formed against thee shall prosper; and every tongue that shall rise against thee in judgment thou shalt condemn. This is the heritage of the servants of the Lord, and their righteousness is of me, saith the Lord.

Isaiah 57:18   I have seen his ways, and will heal him: I will lead him also, and restore comforts unto him and to his mourners.

Isaiah 58:8   Then shall thy light break forth as the morning, and thine health shall spring forth speedily: and thy righteousness shall go before thee; the glory of the Lord shall be thy rereward.

Matthew 8:17   That it might be fulfilled which was spoken by Esaias the prophet, saying, Himself took our infirmities, and bare our sicknesses.

Matthew 17:20b   If ye have faith as a grain of mustard seed, ye shall say unto this mountain, Remove hence to yonder place; and it shall remove; and nothing shall be impossible unto you.

Mark 9:23   Jesus said unto him, If thou canst believe, all things are possible to him that believeth.

Mark 10:27   And Jesus looking upon them saith, With men it is impossible, but not with God: for with God all things are possible.

Mark 11:23   For verily I say unto you, That whosoever shall say unto this mountain, Be thou removed, and be thou cast into the sea; and shall not doubt in his heart, but shall believe that those things which he saith shall come to pass; he shall have whatsoever he saith.

Mark 11:24   Therefore I say unto you, What things soever ye desire, when ye pray, believe that ye receive them, and ye shall have them.

Luke 10:19   Behold, I give unto you power to tread on serpents and scorpions, and over all the power of the enemy: and nothing shall by any means hurt you.

Luke 18:27   And he said, The things which are impossible with men are possible with God.

1 Peter 2:24   Who his own self bare our sins in his own body on the tree, that we, being dead to sins, should live unto righteousness: by whose stripes ye were healed.

1 Peter 5:9   Whom resist stedfast in the faith, knowing that the same afflictions are accomplished in your brethren that are in the world.

1 John 4:4   Ye are of God, little children, and have overcome them: because greater is he that is in you, than he that is in the world.

1 John 5:4   For whatsoever is born of God overcometh the world: and this is the victory that overcometh the world, even our faith.

3 John 1:2   Beloved, I wish above all things that thou mayest prosper and be in health, even as thy soul prospereth.

Revelation 12:11   And they overcame him by the blood of the Lamb, and by the word of their testimony; and they loved not their lives unto the death.

SHORT VERSES ON FAITH

Matthew 8:10   When Jesus heard it, he marvelled, and said to them that followed, Verily I say unto you, I have not found so great faith, no, not in Israel.

Matthew 8:26   And he saith unto them, Why are ye fearful, O ye of little faith? Then he arose, and rebuked the winds and the sea; and there was a great calm.

Matthew 9:2   And, behold, they brought to him a man sick of the palsy, lying on a bed: and Jesus seeing their faith said unto the sick of the palsy; Son, be of good cheer; thy sins be forgiven thee.

Matthew 9:22   But Jesus turned him about, and when he saw her, he said, Daughter, be of good comfort; thy faith hath made thee whole. And the woman was made whole from that hour.

Matthew 9:29   Then touched he their eyes, saying, According to your faith be it unto you.

Matthew 13:58   And he did not many mighty works there because of their unbelief.

Matthew 14:31   And immediately Jesus stretched forth his hand, and caught him, and said unto him, O thou of little faith, wherefore didst thou doubt?

Matthew 15:28   Then Jesus answered and said unto her, O woman, great is thy faith: be it unto thee even as thou wilt. And her daughter was made whole from that very hour.

Matthew 17:17 Then Jesus answered and said, O faithless and perverse generation, how long shall I be with you? how long shall I suffer you? bring him hither to me.

Matthew 17:20 And Jesus said unto them, Because of your unbelief: for verily I say unto you, If ye have faith as a grain of mustard seed, ye shall say unto this mountain, Remove hence to yonder place; and it shall remove; and nothing shall be impossible unto you.

Matthew 21:21 Jesus answered and said unto them, Verily I say unto you, If ye have faith, and doubt not, ye shall not only do this which is done to the fig tree, but also if ye shall say unto this mountain, Be thou removed, and be thou cast into the sea; it shall be done.

Mark 2:5 When Jesus saw their faith, he said unto the sick of the palsy, Son, thy sins be forgiven thee.

Mark 4:40 And he said unto them, Why are ye so fearful? how is it that ye have no faith?

Mark 5:34 And he said unto her, Daughter, thy faith hath made thee whole; go in peace, and be whole of thy plague.

Mark 10:52 And Jesus said unto him, Go thy way; thy faith hath made thee whole. And immediately he received his sight, and followed Jesus in the way.

Mark 11:22 And Jesus answering saith unto them, Have faith in God.

Luke 5:20 And when he saw their faith, he said unto him, Man, thy sins are forgiven thee.

Luke 7:9   When Jesus heard these things, he marvelled at him, and turned him about, and said unto the people that followed him, I say unto you, I have not found so great faith, no, not in Israel.

Luke 7:50   And he said to the woman, Thy faith hath saved thee; go in peace.

Luke 8:48   And he said unto her, Daughter, be of good comfort: thy faith hath made thee whole; go in peace.

Luke 9:41   And Jesus answering said, O faithless and perverse generation, how long shall I be with you, and suffer you? Bring thy son hither.

Luke 17:19   And he said unto him, Arise, go thy way: thy faith hath made thee whole.

Luke 18:42   And Jesus said unto him, Receive thy sight: thy faith hath saved thee.

Luke 22:32   But I have prayed for thee, that thy faith fail not: and when thou art converted, strengthen thy brethren.

John 20:27   Then saith he to Thomas, Reach hither thy finger, and behold my hands; and reach hither thy hand, and thrust it into my side: and be not faithless, but believing.

Acts 3:16   And his name through faith in his name hath made this man strong, whom ye see and know: yea, the faith which is by him hath given him this perfect soundness in the presence of you all.

Acts 14:9 The same heard Paul speak: who stedfastly beholding him, and perceiving that he had faith to be healed,

Romans 1:17 For therein is the righteousness of God revealed from faith to faith: as it is written, The just shall live by faith.

Romans 4:19-20 And being not weak in faith, he considered not his own body now dead, when he was about an hundred years old, neither yet the deadness of Sarah's womb:[20] He staggered not at the promise of God through unbelief; but was strong in faith, giving glory to God;

Romans 10:17 So then faith cometh by hearing, and hearing by the word of God.

Galatians 3:9 So then they which be of faith are blessed with faithful Abraham.

Ephesians 6:16 Above all, taking the shield of faith, wherewith ye shall be able to quench all the fiery darts of the wicked.

1 Thessalonians 5:8 But let us, who are of the day, be sober, putting on the breastplate of faith and love; and for an helmet, the hope of salvation.

1 Timothy 6:12 Fight the good fight of faith, lay hold on eternal life, whereunto thou art also called, and hast professed a good profession before many witnesses.

Hebrews 4:2 For unto us was the gospel preached, as well as unto them: but the word preached did not profit them, not being mixed with faith in them that heard it.

Hebrews 6:12   That ye be not slothful, but followers of them who through faith and patience inherit the promises.

Hebrews 10:23   Let us hold fast the profession of our faith without wavering; (for he is faithful that promised;)

Hebrews 10:38   Now the just shall live by faith: but if any man draw back, my soul shall have no pleasure in him.

Hebrews 11:1   Now faith is the substance of things hoped for, the evidence of things not seen.

Hebrews 11:6   But without faith it is impossible to please him: for he that cometh to God must believe that he is, and that he is a rewarder of them that diligently seek him.

Hebrews 11:30   By faith the walls of Jericho fell down, after they were compassed about seven days

James 1:3   Knowing this, that the trying of your faith worketh patience.

James 1:6   But let him ask in faith, nothing wavering. For he that wavereth is like a wave of the sea driven with the wind and tossed.

James 2:1   My brethren, have not the faith of our Lord Jesus Christ, the Lord of glory, with respect of persons.

James 2:17 Even so faith, if it hath not works, is dead, being alone.

James 5:15 And the prayer of faith shall save the sick, and the Lord shall raise him up; and if he have committed sins, they shall be forgiven him.

1 Peter 1:21 Who by him do believe in God, that raised him up from the dead, and gave him glory; that your faith and hope might be in God.

1 Peter 5:9 Whom resist stedfast in the faith, knowing that the same afflictions are accomplished in your brethren that are in the world.

2 Peter 1:5 And beside this, giving all diligence, add to your faith virtue; and to virtue knowledge;

1 John 5:4 For whatsoever is born of God overcometh the world: and this is the victory that overcometh the world, even our faith.

Jude 1:20 But ye, beloved, building up yourselves on your most holy faith, praying in the Holy Ghost,

SHORT VERSES ON REBUKING THE DEVIL

Matthew 4:10   Then saith Jesus unto him, Get thee hence, Satan: for it is written, Thou shalt worship the Lord thy God, and him only shalt thou serve.

Matthew 8:31-32   So the devils besought him, saying, If thou cast us out, suffer us to go away into the herd of swine. [32] And he said unto them, Go. And when they were come out, they went into the herd of swine: and, behold, the whole herd of swine ran violently down a steep place into the sea, and perished in the waters.

Matthew 10:1   And when he had called unto him his twelve disciples, he gave them power against unclean spirits, to cast them out, and to heal all manner of sickness and all manner of disease.

Matthew 10:8   Heal the sick, cleanse the lepers, raise the dead, cast out devils: freely ye have received, freely give.

Matthew 16:23   But he turned, and said unto Peter, Get thee behind me, Satan: thou art an offence unto me: for thou savourest not the things that be of God, but those that be of men.

Matthew 28:18-19   And Jesus came and spake unto them, saying, All power is given unto me in heaven and in earth. [19] Go ye therefore, and teach all nations, baptizing them in the name of the Father, and of the Son, and of the Holy Ghost:

Mark 3:15 And to have power to heal sicknesses, and to cast out devils:

Mark 6:7 And he called unto him the twelve, and began to send them forth by two and two; and gave them power over unclean spirits;

Luke 9:49 And John answered and said, Master, we saw one casting out devils in thy name; and we forbad him, because he followeth not with us.

Luke 10:17 And the seventy returned again with joy, saying, Lord, even the devils are subject unto us through thy name.

Luke 10:18 And he said unto them, I beheld Satan as lightning fall from heaven.

Luke 10:19 Behold, I give unto you power to tread on serpents and scorpions, and over all the power of the enemy: and nothing shall by any means hurt you.

Luke 10:20 Notwithstanding in this rejoice not, that the spirits are subject unto you; but rather rejoice, because your names are written in heaven.

Luke 22:31-32 31 And the Lord said, Simon, Simon, behold, Satan hath desired to have you, that he may sift you as wheat: [32] But I have prayed for thee, that thy faith fail not: and when thou art converted, strengthen thy brethren.

John 17:15 I pray not that thou shouldest take them out of the world, but that thou shouldest keep them from the evil.

Acts 8:7   For unclean spirits, crying with loud voice, came out of many that were possessed with them: and many taken with palsies, and that were lame, were healed.

Acts 16:18   And this did she many days. But Paul, being grieved, turned and said to the spirit, I command thee in the name of Jesus Christ to come out of her. And he came out the same hour.

Acts 19:12   So that from his body were brought unto the sick handkerchiefs or aprons, and the diseases departed from them, and the evil spirits went out of them.

Acts 26:18   To open their eyes, and to turn them from darkness to light, and from the power of Satan unto God, that they may receive forgiveness of sins, and inheritance among them which are sanctified by faith that is in me.

Romans 16:20   And the God of peace shall bruise Satan under your feet shortly. The grace of our Lord Jesus Christ be with you. Amen.

2 Corinthians 10:3-4   For though we walk in the flesh, we do not war after the flesh: [4] (For the weapons of our warfare are not carnal, but mighty through God to the pulling down of strong holds;)

2 Corinthians 11:14   And no marvel; for Satan himself is transformed into an angel of light.

Ephesians 4:27   Neither give place to the devil.

Ephesians 6:11   Put on the whole armour of God, that ye may be able to stand against the wiles of the devil.

Ephesians 6:12   For we wrestle not against flesh and blood, but against principalities, against powers, against the rulers of the darkness of this world, against spiritual wickedness in high places.

Colossians 2:15   And having spoiled principalities and powers, he made a shew of them openly, triumphing over them in it.

1 Timothy 5:14   I will therefore that the younger women marry, bear children, guide the house, give none occasion to the adversary to speak reproachfully.

2 Timothy 2:22   Flee also youthful lusts: but follow righteousness, faith, charity, peace, with them that call on the Lord out of a pure heart.

Hebrews 2:14   Forasmuch then as the children are partakers of flesh and blood, he also himself likewise took part of the same; that through death he might destroy him that had the power of death, that is, the devil;

James 4:7   Submit yourselves therefore to God. Resist the devil, and he will flee from you.

1 Peter 5:8-9   Be sober, be vigilant; because your adversary the devil, as a roaring lion, walketh about, seeking whom he may devour: [9] Whom resist stedfast in the faith, knowing that the same afflictions are accomplished in your brethren that are in the world.

1 John 2:13   I write unto you, fathers, because ye have known him that is from the beginning. I write unto you, young men, because ye have overcome the wicked one. I write unto you, little children, because ye have known the Father.

1 John 2:14   I have written unto you, fathers, because ye have known him that is from the beginning. I have written unto you, young men, because ye are strong, and the word of God abideth in you, and ye have overcome the wicked one.

1 John 4:1-2   Beloved, believe not every spirit, but try the spirits whether they are of God: because many false prophets are gone out into the world. [2] Hereby know ye the Spirit of God: Every spirit that confesseth that Jesus Christ is come in the flesh is of God:

1 John 4:4   Ye are of God, little children, and have overcome them: because greater is he that is in you, than he that is in the world.

1 John 5:4   For whatsoever is born of God overcometh the world: and this is the victory that overcometh the world, even our faith.

SHORT VERSES ON PATIENCE

Luke 8:15   But that on the good ground are they, which in an honest and good heart, having heard the word, keep it, and bring forth fruit with patience.

Luke 21:19   In your patience possess ye your souls.

Romans 8:25   But if we hope for that we see not, then do we with patience wait for it.

Romans 15:4   For whatsoever things were written aforetime were written for our learning, that we through patience and comfort of the scriptures might have hope.

2 Corinthians 12:12   Truly the signs of an apostle were wrought among you in all patience, in signs, and wonders, and mighty deeds.

Colossians 1:11   Strengthened with all might, according to his glorious power, unto all patience and longsuffering with joyfulness;

Hebrews 6:12   That ye be not slothful, but followers of them who through faith and patience inherit the promises.

Hebrews 10:36   For ye have need of patience, that, after ye have done the will of God, ye might receive the promise.

James 1:3   Knowing this, that the trying of your faith worketh patience.

James 1:4   But let patience have her perfect work, that ye may be perfect and entire, wanting nothing.

James 5:11   Behold, we count them happy which endure. Ye have heard of the patience of Job, and have seen the end of the Lord; that the Lord is very pitiful, and of tender mercy.

2 Peter 3:15   And account that the longsuffering of our Lord is salvation; even as our beloved brother Paul also according to the wisdom given unto him hath written unto you;

Revelation 2:3   And hast borne, and hast patience, and for my name's sake hast laboured, and hast not fainted.

Revelation 14:12   Here is the patience of the saints: here are they that keep the commandments of God, and the faith of Jesus.

These Bible Healing scriptures were compiled by
Dr Timothy O. with License from Cambridge Publishing
to produce the Authorised Kings James Bible extracts.
The extracts were recorded in sections where
healing was directly or indirectly recorded.
The sections attempted to encapsulate
enough context to convey relevant message.

This is the large print edition;
it is clear and easily readable.

This book was put together with practicality in mind hence the
prayer suggestions after each section,
with additional scripture extracts which cover
healing confessions, healing and faith verses, rebuking the
devil and patience verses.

An easy – to – use Bible healing scriptures

www.ingramcontent.com/pod-product-compliance
Lightning Source LLC
Chambersburg PA
CBHW050511170426
43201CB00013B/1918